LONDON
LIVES

Best wishes,

Terence Jenkins

TERENCE JENKINS

A catalogue record for this book is available
from the British Library

ISBN 978-1-908318-39-8

Published by
Acorn Independent Press
www.acornselfpublishing.com

To those who take the road less travelled

ALSO BY TERENCE JENKINS

Another Man's London

Return: A Collection of Short Stories

Co-Author of *The Book of Penge, Anerley
& Crystal Palace*

ABOUT THE AUTHOR

Terence Jenkins is a London guide, a suitable pastime for a flâneur (a stroller through cities who takes pleasure in discovering hidden corners and untold stories), as can be seen in both this book and his previous title, *Another Man's London*. His chatty, informative, illustrated and not a little opinionated guides to parts of London he has explored are the ideal companions to a stroll in the capital.

When he is not discovering lesser-known London, Terry loves writing – both journalism and short stories some of which are collected in his book *Return*

Terence Jenkins lives in South London and is a lover of books, the theatre, cinema and animals.

CONTENTS

Standing on Greta Garbo	1
Drabs in the Mall	5
Of Mice & Men	11
Cornhill	15
Faithful unto Death – a Heroine & her Dog	21
The Temple	27
The Old Price Riots at Covent Garden Theatre	33
Guess Who I Saw on Millbank Today?	37
He Died a Pauper in 1721	41
The Pedlar & his Dog	45
The Tent	49
Oscar, Orson, Larry & Viv	53
Dancing Queen & Fenland Bishops	59
Gideon Mantell	65
Whittington	71
A London Speciality	75
Pineapples, Breadfruit & Mutiny	79
A Fortuitous Meeting in Deptford	85
Croydon Airport	91
Mid-Winter Celebrations in the Borough	97
Grave Pleasures	101
Rotherhithe: More Than Just a Tunnel	107
Turner, Blake & Benedict Arnold in Battersea	113
Sanctuary	119
Madness, War & Peace in Southwark	123

STANDING ON GRETA GARBO

"Excuse me. Could you move, please? You're standing on Greta Garbo."

I looked down and, sure enough, the elderly American tourist was right. There beneath my scuffed trainers was the solitude-seeking Swede herself, dressed in ancient garb as Melpomene the Muse of Tragedy.

What's all this? I asked myself, for no matter where I moved, I ended up standing on some muse or other portrayed by some famous contemporary person. There was Sir Osbert Sitwell as Apollo and to his right Clive Bell, the critic, posed as Bacchus the God of Wine, and many more of the great and good of the times were dressed as somebody else from history, culture or literature.

Trafalgar Square was laid out on what was once the site of the King's Mews (where the Royal falcons were kept at one time before they became the Royal stables). At the north side of the Square is the National Gallery, founded in 1824 at the instigation of George IV and originally in the Pall Mall house of John Julius Angerstein, the Russian philanthropist whose gift of his paintings formed the core of the original national collection. It was not until 1832-1838 that William Wilkins constructed the purpose-built gallery that, although greatly enlarged since, we see today

The National Gallery

*The Swedish Actress, Greta Garbo, dressed as Melpomene,
the Muse of Tragedy*

galleries in the World, some say the greatest, having within its walls some of the finest paintings of Western Europe from 1200 to 1900. In his book, *Britain's Best Museums and Galleries,* Mark Fisher gives it five stars.

It is perhaps in anticipation of such riches that most people ascend the steps to the impressive portico, enter the doors and begin to climb the grand staircase to the central hall and the rest of the galleries. They are too engaged in looking up to look down, as was I, to see the riches beneath their feet.

Boris Anrep (1885-1969), a Russian, like Angerstein, was, perhaps, the foremost mosaicist of his time. A friend of artists such as Augustus John and intellectuals such as the economist Maynard Keynes, he was engaged to cover the floors of the main entrance spaces of the gallery with mosaics. He had already completed the mosaic floor of the Blake room in the Tate Gallery and it may be that this commission led to that of the National Gallery.

He had a lot of space to cover and, whilst the first mosaic was completed in 1928, it was not until 1952 that the last was finished. There are four areas: the Half-Way landing shows "The Awakening of the Muses" where we find Garbo, Bell and Sitwell (already mentioned) along with people who may have been known then but who are forgotten now, such as Maria Volkova (Anrep's sister-in-law) as the classical muses; on the West Vestibule floor we have "The Labours of Life" – a sculptor modelling a statue which represents Art, a woman washing a pig which represents farming and so on, covering twelve human endeavours; the East Vestibule is a bit more jolly and shows us "The Pleasures of Life", there are twelve pleasure in all, including a Christmas pudding, cricket, football, making mud pies and, controversially ambiguous, "Profane Love" which shows a young man and two girls . . . plus a dog!

It is not until we get to the North Vestibule at the top of the staircase where "The Modern Virtues" are depicted that we might see people we recognize. There's T. S. Eliot as Leisure; Lord Rutherford as Curiosity, splitting the atom; and slap bang in the middle in his recognisable blue boiler-suit is Winston Leonard Spenser Churchill, Prime Minister of the United Kingdom (1940-5 and 1951-5) as Defiance. How appropriate for the man who got us through the Second World War. I bet no one stands on him, there'd be hell to pay.

Anrep did not mind his work being walked on for he believed it made a physical contact between the walker and the mosaic that is absent when you view a picture on a wall from a distance. So, next time you're hurrying to see the Leonardo or the Raphael, the Manet or the Delacroix, watch where you are treading for beneath your feet are treasures too.

DRABS IN THE MALL

It's not the kind of thing you expect in The Mall on a cold, bright January Sunday morning, but there, approaching me along the traffic-free processional route from Trafalgar Square to Buckingham Palace were half a dozen women dressed as sixteenth century peasants. If I'd had a hat on I would have doffed it and said something like, "Good morrow, wenches. Whither goest thou and what art thou about at this early hour?". The spell was broken when one of them took out a packet of cigarettes from beneath her capacious pinafore and asked me for a light. I could not oblige but we fell into step and struck up a conversation.

"We're drabs," one of them said and when I looked blank, she went on, "Drabs, you know, hoyden, sluts, camp-followers . . . whores." And then I remembered where I'd come across the word before. One of the witches in *Macbeth* when mixing her hellish broth had cast into the cauldron

"Finger of birth-strangled babe
Ditch delivered by a drab"

Funny how these things come back to you.

"If you're camp-followers, where's the camp?"

One of them pointed up ahead and coming out of

Marlborough Road, beside Saint James's Palace, was a group of men in full contemporary uniform, carrying pikestaffs followed by other Royalist soldiers and nobility.

"We're assembling for the march to Whitehall."

And it was then that everything clicked into place.

In a nation with a reputation for pageantry, its capital, London, plays its part and has many ancient customs and ceremonies that continue to the present day. Some, such as the Lord Mayor's Show in November, the State Opening of Parliament in the same month and Trooping the Colour (the Queen's Birthday Parade in June), attract not only locals but national and international tourists. However, there are other less well-known ceremonies, such as the Trial of the Pyx, in February or March, and the Presentation of the Knollys Rose, on or near June 24th, which also brings Britain's long and colourful history to life. Another such is the Commemoration of the Trial and Execution of Charles I, King and Martyr on Tuesday, January 30th 1649.

Charles, Duke of York, grandson of the executed Mary, Queen of Scots, was not born to be king. He was the second son of King James I and his older brother, Henry, Prince of Wales was heir to the throne. Unfortunately, Henry, a gifted, intelligent young man of great promise, died of typhoid fever when he was just 18, leaving Charles as next-in-line to the throne and in 1625, at the age of 25, upon the death of his father, he became King of Great Britain and Ireland.

He had been a frail child who couldn't walk properly and, like his brother Henry, he too had a speech impediment, a stammer which he was to retain all his life. He learnt

In Whitehall, outside the Banqueting House, from which Charles stepped to his beheading, members of The King's Army commemorate his death. The procession has come from St James' Palace to the place of execution where a service is held.

The bust of Charles I at the Banquette House, Whitehall, where he was executed (left). On the pedestal of the equestrian statue of Charles I is a wreath from The King's Army, a loyalist Stuart re-enactmet society (right)

7

languages quickly and was proficient in French, Italian, Greek and Latin. It is claimed that he inherited his love of the arts from his mother, Anne of Denmark. He built up one of the great art collections of Europe.

Unfortunately, this, along with many other expenses, stretched his income beyond his means. His inability to adjust his way of living was a constant source of friction with Parliament who were loathe to finance his lifestyle. It was this, combined with the issues of raising taxes and those of Parliamentary rights and Charles' religious policies that led to the Civil War. And we all know how that ended, with Charles being led from St James' Palace on a bitter January morning, accompanied by Bishop Juxton and Colonel Thomlinson, his jailer, through the park, across Horse Guards Parade into Whitehall where he was taken into the Banqueting Hall of the old palace. At about two o'clock, he stepped through one of the large, elegant windows onto the scaffold erected outside and met Geoffrey Brandon, the heavily disguised executioner.

The king made a brief speech to the crowd, telling them that he "died a martyr" and "a Christian according to the profession of the Church of England". He was going, he said "from a corruptible to an incorruptible crown". He laid his head on the block and told the executioner to strike "when I put my arms out". He made the sign and, with one stroke, was beheaded. His head was held up for all to see. A great groan went up from the crowd, many of whom pushed forward to dip their handkerchiefs in the royal blood.

Each year, on or near the date of Charles I's execution, January 30th, there are services and ceremonies held in

London by Stuart loyalist groups. The Society of King Charles the Martyr has a short service at the scene of the execution, Banqueting House, where a wreath is laid beneath a bust of the King which surmounts the north-west door. The Royal Martyr Church Union holds a service in the nearby church of St Martin-in-the-Fields and then processes to the equestrian statue of the King on Trafalgar Square where a wreath is laid. Another is placed by the Royal Stuart Society.

The King's Army, one of the English Civil War Society enactment groups and an umbrella term for regiments loyal to the memory of King, follow the route taken by the doomed monarch Charles I. It was this group that my drabs were following. As did I on that bitter winter morning for it is a poignant sight and shows that the House of Stuart can still arouse fierce loyalty.

OF MEN AND MICE

As everyone knows, there are no roads in the Square Mile of the City of London. As part of its Roman heritage, there are streets, alleys and lanes. Philpot Lane is one of the latter, at present an undistinguished cut-through between the A100, Eastcheap, to the south and the A1212, Fenchurch Street, to the north. It's a short-cut from London Bridge to workplaces beyond Leadenhall Market where meat, poultry and fish could once be bought, but which now seems to be full of wine-bars and trendy clothes shops.

In his famous diary Samuel Pepys writes, on Tuesday 28th August 1666:

"At noon I, with my wife and Mercer, to Philpot Lane, a great cook's shop, to the wedding of Mr. Longcracke, a good sober man . . . "

Sam would be pleased to know that he can still find some good places to eat in Philpot Lane, mainly Indian and South Asian restaurants, but gone are the days when the East India Company had one of its sites there. Gone is No.17, the house of Richard Oswald, a main partner in the consortium Grant, Oswald & Co. that owned the Bance Island slave factory in Sierra Leone which provided him with enough riches to buy a Scottish estate and become a laird.

Philpot Lane/Eastcheap – This is the building on which the mice can be found (left) and the two mice (right)

The whole area saw the birth of this shameful trade, for in nearby Mincing Lane, John Hawkins planned the first English slavery trips to Africa, encouraged by Queen Elizabeth I, and Francis Baring of the eponymous Bank which helped to finance it, had a house there.

Gone too is St Dionis Backchurch where Pepys sometimes worshipped. This small, rich City church was destroyed in the Great Fire of 1666 and rebuilt by Wren at the cost of £5,737, 10 shillings and 8 pence. However, as with so many places of worship where there is depopulation because of change, it became redundant and was demolished in 1878. The site was sold and St. Dionis, Parsons Green was built on the proceeds.

The lane, named after Sir John Philpot, Lord Mayor of London 1378-9 who owned land in the area, is a scene of development, like many other places in the City it seems like a permanent building site. When I was there last, one side had been almost completely demolished and all that remained at the southern end was the corner block, No.23 Eastcheap. The building was originally a spice merchant's shop but is now a Caffè Nero. It is an elaborately decorated building and worth a closer look, not simply for its polychromatic, Italianate style but for a small detail on the Philpot Lane side. Most people don't look up when they walk, but if they were to glance up at the building they would see two mice nibbling at or carrying off a chunk of cheese. And thereby hangs a tale (or should that be "tail"?)

One lunchtime, when the building was being constructed, one of the men quarrelled with another and accused him of stealing his cheese. A fight broke out and one of the men fell from the scaffolding and was killed. It was afterwards discovered that mice were responsible. Apocryphal? Might be. But it makes a good story. And why else would the mice be there, half way up a wall, nibbling cheese? A memorial to their dead workmates, perhaps? It certainly makes you remember Philpot Lane which has little else to recommend it.

CORNHILL

The Square Mile of the City of London is the financial hub of the United Kingdom and one of the chief centres of world trade and finance. Cornhill, at its heart, with the Bank of England as a near neighbour, is the highest hill in the City (the other being Ludgate) and rises above the Walbrook, one of the lost rivers of London, which now runs beneath the streets. Cornhill got its name from the grain market which was held there in medieval times.

It is a busy, commercial street with a long, eventful history. At its eastern end, in what is now Leadenhall Street, the Romans built a basilica. St Peter's-upon-Cornhill lays claim to being the first Christian church in London (rebuilt by Sir Christopher Wren and his pupil, Nicholas Hawksmoor). It had a public oven where tenants of the Bishop of London were compelled to bake their bread and pay "oven dues". London's emergence as a centre for banking and insurance began in the coffee houses and taverns of Cornhill. However, what is not generally appreciated are the many literary associations of the area.

Thomas Guy (1644-1724), bookseller and philanthropist, had his bookshop on Cornhill. He made his fortune not only by selling his shares in the South Sea Scheme before the bubble burst, but also by importing, printing and selling bibles. He was a governor of St Thomas' Hospital in Southwark and when it became overcrowded and inadequate, he established Guy's Hospital. Books helped make his fortune and he used it well to benefit his fellow Londoners.

Cornhill was a place to be avoided by those who fell foul of the law for in its length could be found "The Tun" (a notorious prison), the stocks and a pillory. It was in the latter that Daniel Defoe (1660-1731) found himself at one time. He had been educated for the non-conformist ministry but owned a hosiery shop, near Cornhill. He was interested in socio-political matters and it was for publishing the satirical *The Shortest Way with Dissenters* (1702) that earned him a fine, a stay in the Cornhill pillory and some time in Newgate Gaol. He went on to become a secret agent for Tory politician Robert Harley before turning his hand to fiction, making his name with *Robinson Crusoe, A Journal of the Plague Year, Moll Flanders* and his three volume travel book, *A Tour Through the Whole Island of Great Britain.*

One of the most quoted poems in the English language is *Elegy Written in a Country Churchyard* (1751) and its author, Thomas Gray (1716-1771), precursor of the Romantic poets, was born in Cornhill where now stands a bank which bears a bronze plaque of the poet and the line "The curfew tolls the knell of parting day", a fitting quote from his memorable contemplation of death. Although his works are few in number, the other famous ones perhaps being two of his odes, *Ode on a Distant Prospect of Eton College* and *Ode on a Favourite Cat Drowned in a Bowl of Goldfish.* He was offered the post of Poet Laureate which he declined, instead he became Professor of History and Modern Languages at Cambridge.

The plaque to Thomas Gray, poet & author of Elegy Written in a Country Courtyard (left). On the main door of 32 Cornhill, the eighth panel shows the Brontë sisters and Thackeray visiting their publishers: Smith, Elder & Co.

A contemporary of Gray was William Cowper (1731-1800) who, at one time, lived in Cornhill. Although he trained as a lawyer, he never practised. He was also a hymn writer but he is best remembered for his poem *John Gilpin*. Because of his interest in Nature and his writing about such themes, he too is regarded as a forerunner of the better-known Romantic poets such as William Wordsworth. He was of unsound mind and tried to commit suicide in 1763.

The ubiquitous Charles Dickens (1812-1870) made London his own. The picture most people have of "literary" London is his, and Cornhill plays its part here too. In the maze of alleyways leading off the main street is *The George and Vulture* tavern which was a hostelry for Mr. Pickwick during the trial of Bardell *v.* Pickwick. In *A Christmas Carol* the bell of St Michael's church "was always peeping down at Scrooge out of a Gothic window in the wall." It was his use of recognizable detail as well as the memorable characters that brought Dickens' novels to life.

For almost fifty years in the nineteenth century, the publishers, Smith, Elder & Co. had their offices at 65 Cornhill (now No.32). Among their more successful authors were Leigh Hunt, Mrs Gaskell and William Makepeace Thackeray, some of whose novels satirised society and snobbery and one of which, *Vanity Fair*, gave us Becky Sharp, the social-climbing heroine. Thackeray was also editor of the influential *Cornhill Magazine* which was published from the same address.

It was a long journey from the harsh beauty of the Yorkshire moors and the cobbled streets of Haworth to the thriving, commercial thoroughfare in the centre of financial London but it was one which two of the three novelist daughters of the Rev. Patrick Brontë made in 1847. Charlotte, Emily and Anne had written under the pseudonyms of Currer, Ellis and Acton Bell. Their novels, *Jane Eyre*, *Wuthering Heights*, *Agnes Grey* and others had been very successful but not even their publishers, Smith, Elder & Co., knew whether the names were real or assumed, if the authors were one person or more or even if they were men or women. Finally, in 1747, Charlotte and Anne came to the capital where, among other famous people, they met Thackeray at their publishers. During their stay in London they were welcomed in polite society despite the fact that when *Jane Eyre* was published there were those who saw strong sexual elements in it and deemed the novel unsuitable for young ladies.

Cornhill Insurance, the firm which now occupies No.32, has hand-carved panels on their front door, illustrating the history of this busy street. We can see the market, the *Pope's Head* tavern, *Garraway's Coffee House* (which Defoe used to visit) and, in the bottom right-hand corner, are Charlotte and Anne Brontë meeting Thackeray, a fitting reminder of Cornhill's long and many literary associations.

FAITHFUL UNTO DEATH
A HEROINE AND HER DOG

Throughout British history there have been women whose courage has shone like a beacon and has been an example and inspiration to others. Think of Boudicca, warrior Queen of the Iceni, who, according to Tacitus the Roman historian, was flogged by the pillaging and looting Roman army and had to watch as her daughters were raped. She led her army in rebellion against the occupiers, taking Verulamium (St Albans), Camulodunum (Colchester) and Londinium (London). She lay waste to these cities and slew 70,000 Romans. Eventually, in A.D.61 the Roman army won but Boudicca, rather than let herself be captured, took poison. Her bronze statue by Thomas Thorneycroft stands at the north end of Westminster bridge, a reminder, if one were needed, of British pride. "Boudicca" is Celtic for Victory.

Another, humbler, example of female bravery is Grace Darling (1815-1842), the Northumberland lass (born in Bamburgh), who, with her father, was a keeper of the Longstone Lighthouse on one of the Farne Islands. On September 7th 1838, at the height of a raging storm, Grace and her father rowed out and rescued the survivors of the *Forfarshire*, a steamship going from Hull to Dundee, which had broken up on Harker's Rock. Nine people were rescued including a mother who was found clinging to the bodies of her two dead children. The image of this 22 year old girl taking to the huge seas to help others with no thought to her own safety captured the imagination and hearts of the British public. Grace was awarded the Gold Medallion of the Royal Humane Society and the Silver Medal of the Royal National Institute for the Preservation of Life from Shipwreck. She took none of the considerable sums of money that were raised for her by subscription. A heroine, indeed.

In St Martin's Lane in London, on a traffic island between the National Portrait Gallery and the church of St Martin-in-the-Field is the statue of another British heroine who, though not remembered by many today, was the focus of both British and international admiration and respect in 1915 and the years following the First World War.

Like Boudicca, another East Anglian heroine, Edith Cavell was born in Norfolk in 1865, the daughter of a clergyman. After working as a governess in Brussels for four years, she entered the London Hospital as a probationary nurse in 1890 and by 1895 she had become staff nurse. Because of her knowledge of Brussels and foreign languages, in addition to her English nursing experience which was held in high esteem, she was asked back to the city to establish a training school for nurses in 1906. She was soon promoted, becoming Matron of the Berkendael Institute in 1907.

When Belgium was invaded in 1914 she did much work for the Red Cross and treated not only Allied wounded but German as well. She was compassionate and efficient with

*In St Martins Place, is this statue to the nurse, Edith Cavell (1865-1915),
who was executed by the Germans for spying and helping British and French
soldiers to escape. The statue was unveiled by Queen Alexandra.*

a smile that did much to relieve the distress of the patients,
injured and away from home. She was also fond of
animals, especially dogs, and there is a photograph of her
in her garden with two dogs in the Imperial War Museum.
In Brussels she had a cross-bred mutt, mainly Alsatian,
called Jack who followed her around. It may well be that
the injured men were comforted by his friendly presence.
However, in 1915, she was arrested by the Germans and

Jack, the pet of Edith Carvell. After his mistress' execution by firing squad, was rescued by Princes Mary de Croy and taken to her estate in Belgium where he died in 1923 . He was embalmed and returned to England. He is now in the Imperial War Museum.

charged with aiding French and British soldiers to escape and thereby return to their units to continue to fight against them. Cavell had indeed hidden about six hundred soldiers in a variety of places, safe houses and hospitals and had helped them to contact their compatriots. She never denied what she had done and after ten weeks in prison, she was able to accept the German verdict with some equanimity when she was condemned to be executed by firing squad.

While in prison, she was visited by the only remaining English priest, the Rev. Gahan who found her calm and prepared. She said that death brought no fears and "Standing as I do in the view of God and Eternity, I realise that patriotism is not enough. I must have no hatred or bitterness in my heart for anyone" These noble words were inscribed on the memorial statue of Nurse Edith Cavell which was erected by public subscription, for at dawn on October 12th. 1915 she was executed and her body was returned to England for a funeral service in Westminster Abbey. King George V attended and the route was lined by silent thousands. Her body was then sent for burial in Norfolk Cathedral for she was a Norfolk lass.

Along with Edith, others charged with similar offences, including two other women, were reprieved when the King of Spain and the Pope made personal appeals to the Kaiser. After her execution, recruitment into the armed forces rose in Britain; and there was revulsion at what the Germans had done – shot a woman.

And what of Jack, her faithful canine friend? A Belgian aristocrat, Princess Mary de Croy rescued him and took him back to her family estate in Belgium where he lived until 1923. His embalmed body was returned to the care of the Norfolk Red Cross who eventually gave it to the Imperial War Museum in London where, along with other Cavell memorabilia, he can be found downstairs in the section devoted to the First World War.

On the top of the Cavell statue in St Martin's Lane are carved the words, "*Faithful unto Death*", appropriate for both the mistress and her pet.

THE TEMPLE

It has been claimed that London is made up of the City of Westminster, (the seat of government), the City of London (the ancient heart of the capital and a global financial centre), and The Temple. Between the busyness of Fleet Street and the through traffic of the Victoria Embankment is one of London's best kept secrets, 20 acres of ancient buildings, gas-lit alleys and the third largest private garden in the capital (after those of Buckingham and Lambeth Palaces) and all this is redolent with history.

The Temple is home to two of the four Inns of Court, the Middle and Inner Temple (the others being Lincoln's Inn and Gray's Inn) and one of the jewels in its architectural crown, the Temple Church itself. In 1608 King James I granted the freehold of the land to the two resident, but separate, legal institutions on condition that they accommodate and educate students of the law and maintain the Temple Church and its Master.

The Temple is largely free of local and governmental interference and jealously guards this freedom. It is no wonder that Dickens, who lived in nearby Doughty St, wrote in *Barnaby Rudge*, "Who enters here leaves noise behind" and Wordsworth described this place where lawyers live, work and "Look out on waters, walks and gardens green".

Although granted its Charter in 1608, the origin of The Temple goes back much further to the Knights Templar, warrior monks who protected pilgrims to the Holy Land in the twelfth and thirteenth centuries. It was they who built the original temple, round in shape in imitation of the circular Church of the Holy Sepulchre in Jerusalem. It was consecrated by Heraclius, the Patriarch of that city in the presence of King Henry II.

The Knights Templar became a wealthy and powerful force to be reckoned with, owing allegiance only to the Pope. As such, it attracted the attention of Phillip the Fair, King of France (1268-1314) whose coffers needed refilling and whose power needed a boost. He persuaded the Vatican to abolish the Order on the grounds of blasphemy and sodomy. The lands and buildings of the Order were confiscated and given to the Knights Hospitallers who leased The Temple to lawyers for use as a hostel, thus establishing the legal connection which has remained ever since. In 1539 as part of his seizure of church lands King Henry VIII took possession of The Temple and it remained in Royal ownership until the first Stuart monarch gave it its freedom in 1608.

The Temple is a labyrinth but each Inn has its own insignia. The Middle Temple which is west of Middle Temple Lane has a lamb and flag as its crest which adorns doorways and gas lamps. Its distinguished members have included Henry Fielding the novelist and author of *Tom Jones*, the diarist and landscape gardener, John Evelyn, and Sir Francis Drake the courtier and navigator.

Perhaps Middle Temple's greatest treasure is its Hall, built in 1570. Here on February 2nd, 1601 *Twelfth Night* was

The Temple Church built by the Knights Templar – crusading monks – in the twelfth century. It was built round in imitation of the Church of the Holy Sepulchure and was consecrated in 1185 by Heraclius, Patriarch of Jerusalem (left). An effigy of William Marshall, 1st Earl of Pembroke, in the Temple Church (right)

performed for the first time before Gloriana herself, Queen Elizabeth I. It is thought by some that Shakespeare may have been in the cast – just imagine having the two luminaries of the age under one roof!

Among its other treasures is the long Bench Table made from an enormous oak which, after being felled on the order of Good Queen Bess at Windsor, was floated down the River Thames to the hall. The small table in front of it on which barristers must sign the roll is known as "The Cupboard" and was the hatch on Drake's ship, *The Golden Hind.*

Suits of armour and busts of Caesars are on the surrounding walls and in the stained-glass Treasurers' Window, full of coats of arms, are those of Josephus Jekyll above that of Robertus Hyde. Robert Louis Stevenson was a student here and you can imagine him, lost in thought about a tale that was forming in his mind over dinner one evening, idly looking up and seeing the two names for his memorable but damned creation. History is everywhere – even Middle Temple Gardens which stretch down to the Embankment and were the scene, so it is said, of the fatal plucking of the white rose of York and the red rose of Lancaster which are associated with the civil wars between 1455-1485, known to all as the Wars of the Roses.

The Inner Temple has the winged Pegasus as its crest. Its Hall is much more modern, dating from 1955 but there were other halls before that, including the original medieval hall of the Knights Templar. The Library suffered much damage and loss of books during the Blitz of World War II. However, brother lawyers in other countries such as the U.S.A., and Commonwealth members came to its aid after the war and helped to replace book stocks.

King's Bench Walk owes much of its restrained elegance to the design of Sir Christopher Wren. Behind its harmonious facade have lived Vita Sackville-West and her husband, Sir Harold Nicolson, who used No.4 as their London home when not at Sissinghurst Castle in Kent. Oliver Goldsmith lived at No.3 and *She Stoops to Conquer* was written there. Rider Haggard, author of *King Solomon's Mines* and *She* lived at No.13. Charles Lamb lived in Mitre Court Buildings where he looked after his sister Mary upon her release from the insane asylum where she'd been sent for murdering their mother in fit of madness. Samuel Johnson, the great lexicographer and wit, lived at No.1 Inner Temple Lane and James Boswell, his biographer, entered chambers in Farrer's Building to be close to his friend.

The Inner Temple also has its political alumni. The architects of Indian independence and the foundation of Pakistan were four of its members; Mohandas Gandhi, Jawaharlal Nehru, Mohammed Ali Jinnah and Clement Atlee.

The Inns gardens were home to the Royal Horticultural Society's Great Spring Show from 1888 to 1913, before it moved to the Royal Hospital grounds at Chelsea where it became known as the Chelsea Flower Show, now a staple of the Summer Season in the capital.

Dan Brown's book *The Da Vinci Code* and the subsequent film have brought The Temple and its Church to the attention of many and visitors have increased. But having survived the extermination of the Knights Templar, Henry VIII's dissolution of the Knights Hospitallers, the Great Fire of London and the Blitz of World War II, I'm sure its "Reverend and Valiant Master", can handle the influx of tourists curious to find out more about the church founded by the "*Poor Fellow-Soldiers of Christ and of the Temple of Solomon*" in 1118.

THE OLD PRICE RIOTS AT
COVENT GARDEN THEATRE

If actors today think they have a hard time when they receive bad reviews, they ought to be thankful they didn't live and perform at a time when criticism was more concrete. Eighteenth and nineteenth century London saw frequent theatre riots. In 1749 the New Theatre, Haymarket, was almost destroyed when the audience, used to being titillated by theatrical spectacles, was disappointed to such an extent with the non-appearance of a promised display, the production of a man from a bottle.

When the famous actor-manager David Garrick tried to do away with the cheaper seats for those arriving at Covent Garden after half-time, the audience rioted and damaged the theatre to such an extent that Garrick capitulated and reinstated the cheaper prices. An incensed audience was no respecter of property or person. Once, when King George II and Queen Caroline were at Drury Lane, the theatre was almost demolished and their Majesties beat an early retreat.

Perhaps the most famous, and certainly the largest and longest riots were those at Covent Garden in 1809. The venue which is now known as The Royal Opera House, but often referred to as "Covent Garden", is not the first theatre

The Royal Opera House, Covent Garden.

on this site. In fact it is the third, following fires in 1808 and 1857 and there was extensive reconstruction work in the 1990's.

In 1808 the second theatre burned down and it wasn't until September 1809 that the new theatre, designed by Robert Smirke, reopened to the public. The actor-manager, John Philip Kemble opened the new season with *Macbeth*, an old favourite. During this time, the program was varied and while operas and ballet were presented, a variety of performances drew in the crowds: Grimaldi the famous clown appeared there in pantomime and there were musical shows as well. However, all was not well when the supposedly cursed "Scottish Play" opened.

The new theatre was bigger and, in an attempt to recoup some the renovation costs, Kemble increased the prices and converted some of the public spaces to private boxes. As if this wasn't enough to incite a public which had gone without the Theatre Royal for a year or so, the view from the Gallery was so bad that only the actors' legs could be seen.

The play was booed and hissed and there were constant cries of "Old prices, old prices". The stars, Kemble himself as Macbeth and his sister, the great tragedienne, Sarah Siddons, were forced to leave the stage. The show ended early and 500 soldiers were called in to quell the rioters but with no success. Many of the rioters simply climbed down to the lower galleries and continued their disruption from there. More help was sought by Kemble when he called in the police from Bow Street station across the road but this only antagonised the rioters more and it was not until the early hours of the morning that they dispersed.

For weeks this continued with rioters carrying banners, pigs let loose in the theatre and a magistrate reading the Riot Act from one of the boxes – to no avail for he too was booed and hissed. A coffin inscribed 'The Body of New Prices" was carried round the auditorium. People proudly wore "Old Price" badges and were greeted with warmth as veterans of the ongoing war between management and the public. A special "War Dance" was invented and added to the festivities where men danced in drag and many wore fancy-dress and funny masks. And why not? All this was far more entertaining than the usual fare at the theatre.

The riot was not confined to the theatre. Each evening, after whatever show they had disrupted, the rioters would sing and dance through the streets, always ending up at Kemble's house where they blew whistles, booed and hissed and chanted "Old prices, old prices". However, unlike other riots, this one caused no damage to the theatre itself (though it did little for Kemble's reputation). In fact, there was an air of good humoured jollity about the whole affair. The rioters determined to gain their aim by perseverance rather than brute force and intimidation.

This continued for almost three months until Kemble gave in, reduced the prices and apologised. The rioters were satisfied and the Old Price war ended . . . for the present. Foolishly, Kemble broke his promise the next season when he tried to keep the private boxes. The riots started again and, once more Kemble gave in. He should have been thankful that, unlike previous riots when the theatre had been damaged, Covent Garden remained unscathed even though it didn't prove very profitable. So, next time you go to see *Les Sylphides* or *The Force of Destiny* in your best bib and tucker, you may hear faint echoes of "Old prices, old prices" amid the air-kissing and champagne drinking in the Crush Bar.

GUESS WHO I SAW ON MILLBANK TODAY?

If you stand on Lambeth Bridge at low tide you can see two small shingle beaches emerging from the murky waters of the Thames, one on each side of the river. These must have been a welcome sight to the Romans long ago, as they tramped along the river's edge looking for somewhere shallow enough to cross to progress in their new province of Britannia. This ford was the reason for the development of Lambeth on the southern side and what we now call Millbank on the northern, so called because Westminster Abbey mill once stood on what is now Great College Street.

Millbank, which runs from Vauxhall Bridge almost to Parliament Square, ending at Abingdon Street, has had, and still has, some remarkable buildings along its length. At one time, in the late eighteenth and ninteenth centuries, the octagonal-shaped penitentiary built according to Jeremy Bentham's ideas in his *The Panopticon or Inspection House* was there, where those unfortunates sentenced to being sent to Australia as punishment were imprisoned. It was not until 1890 that it was closed and the Tate Gallery, now a treasure house of British art, was built on the site.

At the other end, at number 1, is the building which once housed the Church Commissioners but which is now Parliamentary offices. In between, standing at the north end of Lambeth Bridge like a pair of not quite matching

The main doors to number 9 Millbank – once ICI offices at Group Headquarters – showing the twelve three dimensional panels. The doors are open and closed electronically.

Panel 12 – Michael Faraday gives a lecture at the Royal Institution. Several contemporary scientists are shown in the front row. Left to right are: Tyndall, Huxley, Darwin, Wheatstone, Crookes, Daniels and Frankland.

book-ends are the headquarters of MI5, on the west side of Horseferry Road, (It seems daft to me. What's the point of being a spy if everyone knows your address?) And, on the east side, ICI House, No.9, Millbank, once the home of the now defunct chemical conglomerate company which has become government offices.

The building, designed by Sir Frank Baines, is handsome and monumental. The Grade Two-listed facade has some interesting external decorations by the sculptor Charles Sergeant Jagger. There are allegorical figures of The Builder, Marine Transport, Agriculture and, fittingly, Chemistry, plus shells, peacocks and the heads of those associated with the development of the chemical industries, Mond, Nobel and others. But it is the main doors which are worthy of special interest and which largely goes unseen by passers-by.

The 20ft-high doors are very much like the famous Ghiberti doors on the Baptistery in Florence. Each door weighs two and a half tons and they have to be opened electronically. There are no locks. Made of bronze and sprayed with a nickel copper alloy, they have six panels each of which show a kind of "before" and "since" sequence of the progress of science and industry. The left hand doors depict primitive man hunting, engaged in agriculture, transport and various crafts. The panels on the right hand door show how these activities have developed science. The modeller of the doors, W. B. Fagan, has put himself in panel No.2 on the right which shows Mount Wilson Observatory in California.

But it is one of the panels on the bottom which may arouse the most interest. On the left, we can see primitive man, dressed in skins, engaged in the fundamental task of measuring the duration of the shortest and longest days. The panel on the right shows an occasion at the Royal Institution when Michael Faraday lectured to many distinguished scientists. Sitting in the front row are Tyndall, Huxley, Wheatstone, Crookes, Daniels, Frankland and, third from the left is Charles Darwin, the scientist who changed how Man saw his place in the world with his *Theory of Evolution.*

So, next time you're passing, take time to have a look at the doors and make the acquaintance, albeit in bronze, of the man who changed the world for ever, Charles Darwin, and when you go home that night you can say to the family, "Guess who I saw on Milbank today".

HE DIED A PAUPER IN 1721

What a sad end to come to and what has it to do with the oldest annually contested race in the British sporting calendar?

I once had a headmaster who, at the beginning of each academic year, used to warn the assembled staff and pupils that "The adoration of the masses is a fickle thing". Worth remembering in these days of celebrity culture and the pursuit of Andy Warhol's "fifteen minutes of fame" which he believed was all that was allotted to us. No one illustrates this more than Thomas Doggett. *Who?* I hear you ask, thereby confirming Warhol's theory.

One day after visiting Eltham Palace, SE9, that splendid amalgam of Art Deco, Tudor and previous eras, I decided to find out if Eltham had anything further to offer of interest. After all, it was once an attractive Kentish village on the main road from London to Maidstone but, like so many other places swallowed up by the urban sprawl of the capital, much of that attraction has vanished. I knew that Van Dyck had once lived there and that Bob Hope and Frankie Howerd, both comedians, had been born there but I wanted something a little more solid.

On the High Street I found the parish church of St John the Baptist which, though built in 1875, was the latest of a number of churches on the site. The church was closed but a man pottering about the graveyard answered my question, "Anybody famous buried here?" by pointing to the side of the church, where up against the wall I'd find Doggett's grave. The name rang a bell so off I went to look for it. And there, on a piece of wood, not even a tombstone, I found the grave of "Thomas Doggett, Actor and Author/Manager of the Haymarket and Drury Lane Theatres. In 1715 he founded the Race for Doggett's Coat and Badge. He died a pauper in 1721".

That's when things clicked into place. I remembered a pub in Lacy Road, Putney, *The Coat and Badge*, and another one, more central, on the south-west corner of Blackfriars Bridge which had once been called *Doggett's Coat and Badge* but which is now simply called *Doggett's*, a fine place for a pint and a splendid view of Wren's masterpiece, St Paul's cathedral.

Anyway, back to Thomas Doggett. He was an Irish actor and, like Hope and Howerd, was also a comedian (is it something in the Eltham water?). Not only was he successful in this role, but also as manager of the Drury Lane Theatre, (one of the foremost of its day) and, later of the Haymarket Theatre, an equally renowned place of entertainment.

He lived in Chelsea, some distance from his place of work. The Thames was, in those days, a major London highway and the river was full of craft, both commercial and private. It was on these that Doggett relied for transport, taking the equivalent of the modern London black taxi, a wherry, down river to the theatres. These shallow, light boats, sharp at

In the churchyard of Eltham Parish Church is the grave of Thomas Doggett.

Doggett's – the riverside pub by Blackfriars Bridge, named after the actor/manager, Thomas Doggett.

both ends, were noted for their speed and the wherry-men used to frequent the landing places, stairs and steps along the river, plying for trade.

It is not known if Doggett used the same wherry-man all the time, but he became friendly with many of them and established a race for apprentice Watermen of the River Thames. One apocryphal story has it that he established the race in gratitude for being saved when falling overboard one time, but it is more likely that it was for the good service and pleasant company he received. The race is 4 miles 5 furlongs between London Bridge and Cadogan Pier, Chelsea. It is held every July and the first prize is a Waterman's red coat with a splendid silver badge on it which is embossed with a horse, (the insignia of the House of Hanover which had acceded to the English throne in 1714). The first race was in 1715. I wonder if George I came to watch or if he understood what was going on for he spoke little or no English.

The race was held each year until Doggett's death in 1721. In his will he left instructions for its continuance and since then it has been organised by the Fishmongers' Company making it the oldest annually contested race in the British sporting calendar. I wonder if it was the expense of the race which caused Doggett to die a pauper, poor chap.

THE PEDLAR & HIS DOG

Opposite the Houses of Parliament, across the River Thames, in South London is Lambeth Palace, the London home of the Archbishops of Canterbury. Next door to the splendid red Tudor brickwork of its gatehouse is St Mary-at-Lambeth, now the Garden Museum.

The church has a long and chequered history and houses the graves of John and Rosemary Nicholson, who saved the garden from demolition in the seventies *(for more information see Pineapples, Breadfruit & Mutiny, p.77)*

Another famous Lambeth resident lies at rest here also, Captain William Bligh who lived at 100 Lambeth Road. In 1787 he was given command of *The Bounty* and it is claimed that his harsh discipline caused a mutiny when Fletcher Christian and other crew members seized the ship. This is not recorded on his tomb.

It is not for these reasons that dog-lovers should visit the Museum, but for someone less famous. In the Middle Ages, one of the parishioners was a local pedlar who sold his wares around the borough and, sometimes, across the river where there was more chance of trade. It was a hard life and, potentially, a lonely one. However, this pedlar was always accompanied by his faithful dog with whom he shared his food. They were inseparable and a well-known

The Pedlar's window in the church of St Mary at Lambeth.

sight, south of the Thames in what was then rural Lambeth. The dog wasn't only a friend, he was useful in scaring off rascals and footpads who lay in wait in dark, lonely places.

Everyone thought the pedlar was poor and didn't have two pennies to rub together, so it came as something of a surprise when he approached the church authorities and made them an offer they couldn't refuse. If they would allow him to be buried with his dog in the churchyard, when the time came, and would commemorate both himself and his canine friend with a window, he would give them an acre of land.

People found it hard to believe that this itinerant salesman and his mutt had such a gift to give. But he did. The deal was made and when the time came, the window was placed in the church wall and the two friends were buried in the churchyard. Unfortunately, the original was destroyed by enemy action in the War. However, a modern window, designed by Francis Stephens, is in the south chapel, showing the pedlar loaded down with his wares and his trusty dog looking up at him. One of the earliest books on dogs, *Of English Dogs* by John Caius, published in 1576, said that there were three types of canines: dogs serving game; homely dogs; currish dogs (which might be trained). The Pedlar's dog looks like a mixture of all three.

Underneath the figures is inscribed "May God prosper the land as he prospered me". God certainly did, for in 1910 when the land was sold to the London County Council for the building of County Hall, it fetched £81,000 a vast sum in those days. It would have kept the faithful dog in bones for ever.

THE TENT

What the Great Fire of London in 1666 and Hitler's bombs in the Second World War Blitz failed to do, the IRA did in 1993 when one of the oldest medieval churches in the City, *St Ethelburga-the-Virgin* within Bishopsgate was completely destroyed by one of their massive bombs.

Probably built in the thirteenth century, it was the smallest of the many City churches and survived the Great Fire which stopped before it reached it. Among its many treasures were three stained glass windows commemorating Henry Hudson and his crew who took communion there before setting out on their voyage to find the North-West Passage in 1607. Some of the windows showed scenes from their adventures in the Americas.

Among its many ministers was John Deye who in 1553, during the reign of Queen Mary (Bloody Mary, the daughter of Henry VIII and Catherine of Aragon), had his ear nailed to the pillory for "heinous words against the Queen's majesty".

Who was this saint with the strange name? In a city with churches dedicated to St Botolph (3) and St Ethldreda (1), we should not be surprised by the oddity of the Saxon name. She was the daughter of Ethelbert, King of Kent who was the first notable convert to Christianity by St Augustine in 597, and sister of St Erkenwald, Bishop of London. She was Abbess of Barking.

The Church of St. Ethelburga–the–Virgin, within Bishopsgate.

Inside the Tent, all faiths are welcome. Their sacred books are laid out for them.

When first built, it was the tallest building in the area but now it is surrounded by skyscrapers such as the Gherkin and what was once called the NatWest Tower. The small, simple, ragstone building with its attractive bell tower and weather vane is dwarfed by these and other towers dedicated to the worship of Mammon.

Although completely destroyed by the I.R.A. bomb and marked for demolition and clearing by the Church of England, there was such public outcry that it was rebuilt to its original plan but the interior and its use is much changed. It is now *St Ethelburga's Centre for Reconciliation and Peace*, an independent charity. While the interior of the building, the nave and aisle, would be recognised by churchgoers, it is outside in the small courtyard at the back that they would be most surprised. For there, sitting in an Andalucian garden is a sixteen-sided Bedouin tent made of goat hair but with stained glass windows.

The Tent was designed by Professor Keith Critchlow, foremost authority on sacred spaces where people of all faiths meet. There is no religious symbolism and on the windows the sun and moon (symbols of reconciliation) are depicted and the word for Peace in inscribed in different languages. The Tent is a centre for partnership and collaboration with a programme of lectures, discussions and prayer meetings organised by a large group of voluntary helpers. Christians, Jews, Muslims, Hindus, Jains and all faiths are welcome at the Tent. In financial London with all its hurry and stress, it is definitely worth finding.

OSCAR, ORSON, LARRY & VIV

On the 5th July 1763 Dr Samuel Johnson told James Boswell that if he wanted to have a proper idea of "the magnitude of London", he must not be satisfied with "its great streets and squares but must survey its innumerable little lanes and courts." Angel Court (SW1) is just the sort of place the great lexicographer was encouraging his young Scottish friend to visit.

The Court runs between Pall Mall and King Street in St James (an area of exclusive gentlemen's clubs and expensive shops), and although most of the grand houses there are now offices, there is still an atmosphere of "Upstairs/Downstairs" about it. Christies is across the road and Spink just up the street. Antique shops and galleries abound. Posh. At one time it may have been a bit more inviting than it is today for modern "development" has robbed it of much of its character and I certainly would not like to go through the Court at night especially if *The Golden Lion*, an excellent pub at one end was closed. But to avoid it altogether would be to miss some of London's theatrical history and the attractive bas-relief panels by E. Bainbridge Copnall that commemorate it.

At one time, the St James Theatre stood on the site. It was built for the famous Victorian tenor John Braham who later became bankrupt. The theatre passed through various ownerships, remodelling and changing names over the years, eventually reverting to its original name – The St James Theatre and entering its most successful phase under the management of George Alexander from 1890 to 1918. It was he who produced the first performance Pinero's *The Second Mrs Tanquery*, a great success.

In 1892 he premiered *Lady Windermere's Fan* by Oscar Wilde, the first of his plays, which led to the Irish wit and author becoming the most successful playwright in Victorian London. On February 14th 1895 he premiered another of Wilde's plays, *The Importance of Being Earnest* which also packed out the theatre. But Wilde's fame was soon to turn to notoriety and downfall for six weeks later on April 1, Oscar was arrested at the Cadogan Hotel and charged with gross indecency, for which he was found guilty and sentenced to two years imprisonment. Poor Oscar ended his life in poverty and exile, dying in Paris and being buried in Pere Lachaise cemetery. Apparently, his grave, after that of Jim Morison, lead singer of The Doors, is the most visited and there are usually flowers laid there by fans.

Sir Gerald du Maurier was actor-manager during the 1930's and 1940's but the most famous of those who later ran the theatre after this are Laurence Olivier and Vivien Leigh who took it over in 1950. Among their first productions was Shakespeare's *Othello*, directed by Orson Welles, who also starred as the Moor.

Welles had gained fame with such productions as the Mercury Theatre's *War of the Worlds* on American radio which was so realistic that it caused panic across the States when people genuinely thought their country was being invaded by aliens. His voodoo version of *Macbeth*, set

The relief of Oscar Wilde, with Dorian Gray and Salome on either side.

The relief outside The Golden Lion, in Angel Court, of Vivien Leigh as Cleopatra – with asp – and Antony, with sword: both about to die.

in Haiti and with an all-black cast was another of his novel attitudes to drama. And, of course, his black and white film, *Citizen Kane*, is recognised today as one of the greatest films of all time.

His approach to *Othello* was no less idiosyncratic. During rehearsals he would shout, "'Act, you sons of bitches, act". He did not participate in the rehearsals himself until just before the opening date and just a week before the curtain was to go up, he vanished for four days. When he showed up, he said that he'd had to go to Venice for a party.

Othello was a success, despite the fact that Welles, a large man who sweated so much that when he and his Desdemona (played by Gudrun Ure), took their curtain calls, she was covered in black greasepaint and looked as though she had been wrestling with a chimney-sweep. The production lasted three months and broke even. Kenneth Tynan, the acerbic critic said that Welles had played Othello 'with the courage of his restrictions'.

Olivier and Leigh themselves starred in some of their own productions. In 1951, for the Festival of Britain, they appeared in Shaw's *Caesar and Cleopatra* and Shakespeare's *Antony and Cleopatra*, both commercial and critical successes. However, in 1957 Gilbert Miller, the American impresario who owned the theatre, put it up for sale and it was scheduled for demolition. There was outcry and protest at this "act of vandalism" (as it was seen by many). Olivier and Leigh not only organised a nation-wide campaign to save it but marched through the streets to the House of Lords with hundreds of people waving banners. All in vain for although the Lords voted against the Government, the

St James Theatre was demolished. In its place an office block was erected and as a sop to its theatrical history and cultural importance, sculptured balcony fronts were placed on each floor above the main entrance with bas-reliefs showing those associated with the theatre. There are Gilbert Miller the one-time owner, George Alexander the producer, Oscar Wilde and the Oliviers. Ironically, this building did not last long and, in 1966, it too was demolished to make way for another modern block which now occupies the space. Fortunately, the reliefs were saved but relegated to the alleyway between the new St James House and *The Golden Lion.*

If you're in a hurry to drop off an heirloom at Christies or to catch a show at The Royal Academy, take a short cut through Angel Court and look for the panels which bear witness to a lost piece of our rich theatrical history. You'll see Cleopatra about to put the asp to her bosom and Antony with his sword ready to commit suicide to avoid capture by Octavius. There too is Oscar flanked by Dorian Gray looking at the damned likeness of his portrait on one side and Salome gloating over the head of John the Baptist on the other. But go while it's light for in the gloaming it's enough to give anyone the willies.

DANCING QUEEN & FENLAND BISHOPS

The last of the Tudor monarchs, Elizabeth I, daughter of that ogre, Henry VIII and the unfortunate Anne Boleyn, was a woman of many parts: queen of a rapidly expanding mercantile empire, multi-lingual Protestant diplomat in a Europe that was largely Catholic and the head and heart of a glittering court where nobles vied for her favour and plotters schemed to be rid of her. A demanding position to fill, indeed, but Gloriana had her lighter moments and diversions from the business of State, some of which were provided by one of her favourites, Sir Christopher Hatton.

Hatton (1540-1591), a handsome and accomplished man, was especially well-known for his dancing which was elegant and seductive enough to attract the attention of the Virgin Queen herself who was fond of a trim ankle and a fair face. He became a regular partner of the Queen in many a sarabande and quadrille and she was not ungrateful for their time together. We can see the results of her generosity in London today.

Hatton Garden, at the edge of the City of London, is now the centre of the diamond trade but it has not always been so. At one time it covered a much wider area when it belonged to the Bishops of Ely who, like many other prelates in mediaeval times, played a more active part in the running of the State and needed to be in the capital to do so. In what is now the London postal district EC1, they built a palace with extensive gardens which were to give their name to the area in future times. Not only were they famous for their size and beauty but also for the fruits they provided, especially strawberries. In Shakespeare's *Richard III*, the Duke of Gloucester mentions the delicious strawberries in the Bishop's garden. Although the fruit gardens have long gone, a *Strawberrie Fayre* is held each year in June.

The Bishops of Ely were powerful churchmen and politicians. One of them entertained Henry VIII and Catherine of Aragon to a series of banquets that lasted almost a week, during which he served, "168 swans and 4,000 larks" among other delicacies. It was gourmandizing on a large scale.

It was to the lands of these Bishops that Elizabeth I looked as a means of rewarding her favourite dance-partner. He was not as blessed with ancestral estates and London homes as some of the aristocracy that attended the Elizabethan court, like bees around a hive, and the Queen rectified this by ordering the then Bishop of Ely to give some land to Hatton. No doubt the prelate was wise enough not to put up opposition. A lease was granted for a payment of "£10 p.a., ten loads of hay and a red rose picked at mid-summer". Hatton must have been doing something right for he went on to become Elizabeth's Lord Chancellor. Some, including Mary, Queen of Scots, claimed that he was her lover. There is no evidence for this. However, Hatton was appointed one of the commissioners who found Mary guilty of treason and sent her, a woman of great beauty and accomplishments, to death by execution.

Inside St. Etheldreda's Church in Ely's Place.

Ely Place's Strawberrie Fayre.

Near the southern end of Hatton Garden is Mitre Court, a narrow alley which leads to the ancient *Mitre Tavern* which claims to be the smallest hostelry

in the capital and always has a warm welcome. *The Mitre* was built by Bishop Goodrich in 1546 for the use of his servants. In one corner, near the door, is the preserved trunk of a cherry tree around which, it is claimed, Good Queen Bess danced with her favourite dancing partner, Christopher Hatton. This small, atmospheric pub is well worth a visit.

If you continue through the alley you will find Ely Place, one of the last private roads in London. It is gated and at one time was supervised by a top-hatted beadle who not only controlled the comings and goings but who would, on the hour, leave his lodge and call out the time. Sadly, this ended with the Second World War. Apparently, the road and the pub are still technically Cambridgeshire and the police may enter only if invited.

In Ely Place, one of the reminders of its ecclesiastical history, is the magnificent Gothic church of Saint Etheldreda which was built in the late thirteenth century as a private chapel for the Bishop. It is named after an Abbess of Ely and, gruesomely, a part of her hand is kept in the church as a holy relic. The church is Britain's oldest surviving Roman Catholic church and has had an unsurprisingly chequered history. After the tribulations of the Reformation, Catholics worshipped here in the seventeeth century under the protection of Gondomar, the Spanish Ambassador who lived in Ely Place. During the Great Fire of London in 1666 only a change of wind saved it from the general conflagration. Although it was used for Anglican worship for many years, it was returned to the Roman Catholics in 1874.

It is a double-decker building, having two chapels, one on top of the other. Both are very beautiful, the crypt being more austere while the upper church with its statues of Catholic martyrs, rich stained glass, Victorian screen and Lewis organ lends itself to worship, meditation and a famous choral tradition. It is a glorious place to hear a service in sung Latin.

On 3rd of February, the Feast of Saint Blaise, the Blessing of the Throats ceremony takes place. Blaise was martyred in the Emperor Diocletian's persecutions. Legend has it that he saved a youth from choking to death with a bone stuck in his throat. At the annual ceremony those with throat diseases come to the church and the priest holds lighted candles near to cure them, sometimes in the form of a cross against the afflicted throat.

Although not so extensive and beautiful as when Elizabeth I and her Lord Chancellor dallied there, Hatton Garden and the nearby streets are full of historic interest, Do visit, even if you haven't a sore throat.

GIDEON MANTELL

Gideon Mantell was born in 1790 in Lewes, Sussex, where he became a surgeon, specialising in midwifery. He was successful at this but his consuming interests were natural history and geology. Living in the Sussex Weald gave him an opportunity to indulge them. One day when out on a house-call with his wife, Mary Ann, she found, in the Lower Cretaceous stones of the Bestede Quarry near Cuckfield, the fossilised teeth of a beast which Mantell called an Iguanodon because its teeth were similar to those of the South American Iguana. Hence the name, which means "iguana tooth".

There has been disagreement about who found the teeth, but in Mantell's papers, discovered long after his death, he states that he himself made the discovery. Perhaps he let his wife take the credit to keep the peace. She eventually left him because the house became full to bursting point with fossils.

Other geologists and palaeontologists made light of the find and Mantell's claims and it was not until 1825 that he plucked up enough courage to write a scientific description. Working with more Iguanodon fossils, he made the first reconstruction of a dinosaur. Only then did the idea of giant terrestrial reptiles over 35ft-high take hold. This brought Mantell and his palaeontology to wider public notice to such an extent that Charles Dickens corresponded with him and used knowledge gained from Mantell's discoveries in his writings. In the opening paragraph of *Bleak House*, Dickens describes the weather conditions being bad enough to imagine meeting a megalosaurus trundling up Holborn Hill in London.

Mantell continued with his studies, building up a famous collection of fossils which he sold to the British Museum for £5,000 (a huge sum in those days). This collection is now in the Natural History Museum.

In 1839 he moved to London. His medical practice declined but his scientific reputation grew. He wrote 48 scientific papers, some of which were published by The Royal Society and The Geological Society (of which he became Vice-President). He was also asked to join the Linnean Society. His final honour was being granted a pension by the Crown. He became a successful lecturer, making the infant sciences of geology and palaeontology popular. Of his 67 books, one, *The Wonders of Science*, ran through six editions in the first ten years of publication.

His later years were marred by pain from a spinal complaint as a result of an accident for which he took opium. By the time of his death, in 1852, he had discovered four of the five genera of known dinosaurs. He is buried in West Norwood Cemetery in South London. His discoveries influenced one of the great celebrations of Victorian England.

In 1851 the Great Exhibition was opened in Hyde Park, in "the first modern building", a gigantic conservatory of 4,000 tons of iron and 400 tons of glass. Joseph Paxton (1803-1865), the architect who had been the head gardener for the Duke of Devonshire, had based the design on a conservatory he had built at Chatsworth, the Duke's Derbyshire Estate.

The grave of Gideon Mantell in West Norwood Cemetery.

An Iguanodon in Crystal Palace Park. Gideon Mantell first discovered the remains of this dinosaur.

The Exhibition was a great success, making enough money to finance the building of the Albert Hall. The building too was such a success that when the Exhibition closed, it was bought by the Crystal Palace Company and transferred to the top of Sydenham Hill in South-East London. There, with modifications and enlargements amid gardens, fountains and lakes, the eminent palaeontologist, Professor Richard Owen, with the backing of Prince Albert, decide to build a dinosaur park.

One of the purposes of the Great Exhibition was educational and this theme was continued in its new home; Owen's plan was to create a section in the park for "Geology and Inhabitants of the Ancient World". There was a cliff showing mountain limestone, millstone grit, bands of ironstone and seams of coal, capped with New Red Sandstone, constructed by thousands of tons of actual materials.

To crown this, there were life-sized models of dinosaurs (a word which Owen himself created). It is Greek for "powerful lizards" and before this time, there was no idea that anything like a dinosaur once roamed the earth. The models were set on islands in the lake showing the various strata of the earth that existed during the dinosaur period. The Megalosaurus was on the Oolite formation, the Ichthyosaurus and Plesiosaurus on the Lias formation and the Dicynodon on the New Red Sandstone. Other, such as the Pterodactyl, the Iguanodon, the Ichthyosaurus and the Giant Sloth were also on their appropriate formations.

There were some inaccuracies in the models. The Iguanodon stands on four pillar-like legs rather than two and an odd spike-liked bone was placed on its nose like a rhino's horn, whereas it is now know that it was a thumb-like digit. It is important to remember that they represent the extent of contemporary Victorian geology and palaeontology. More recent research and discoveries have shown us their mistakes. The body of the Iguanodon, for example, was held horizontally, with its stiff tail off the ground; it walked bipedally or on all fours.

The Victorians were not without a sense of fun. Inside the Iguanodon on New Year's Eve 1853 a banquet was held. Not only was the venue somewhat singular but the invitation were issued on "Pterodactyl wings" and 20 eminent scientists sat down to a rich meal in the bowels of an extinct beasts made of iron columns and hoops, bricks, tiles and crushed stone.

In June 1854 Queen Victoria opened the display and the prehistoric animals were such a success that the term "dinomania" was coined to describe the many thousands of people who flocked to see the extraordinary models. This was more than 100 years before Stephen Spielburg and *Jurassic Park.*

On the 30th November 1936, the Crystal Palace burned down, taking its many treasures with it. The dinosaurs survived, thanks to the durability of Waterhouse Hawkins' work and some careful restoration. If you go to Crystal Palace Park, you will find peering from the lakes, bushes and trees, a collection of prehistoric monsters which retain their Victorian magnificence and bear witness to Gideon Mantell's discoveries in the Sussex Weald. Do visit the world's first dinosaur theme park.

WHITTINGTON

We British have a reputation for being eccentric, especially in our love of animals, such as our pets, cats, dogs, birds and fish, not to mention the rest of the animal world that we support with our charities. Another of our "eccentricities" is the dramatic form of entertainment known as "pantomime" performed at Christmas time for both children and adults alike. This seasonal entertainment developed during the nineteenth century from the harlequinade of the eighteenth. Pantomime includes popular songs, slapstick, topical comedy, sometimes acrobatics and other skills, and much audience participation and joy. We all remember shouting, *"Look behind you."*

Pantos are based on myths, legends, fairy tales and folklore. They obey certain traditions: the Dame, a comic old woman is played by a man, often a comedian known to the audience and the hero/principal boy is always played by a girl, usually one with shapely legs. And, at the end, Good always triumphs.

Often pantomimes tell stories about universally known characters such as Cinderella, Aladdin or Robin Hood and very often they contain animal characters: a pantomime horse, a faithful dog and, in *Dick Whittington*, a loyal cat. There is, however, an historical basis for this last-named panto.

Richard Whittington (1358-1423) was a real person, the youngest son of Sir William Whittington of Pauntley in Gloucestershire. He left home to travel to London where, he hoped, he would find his fortune in "streets paved with gold". In the panto he is accompanied by a sole companion, Puss, a cat with lustrous black fur, who shares his master's travels and adventures. Eventually, it is he who brings about a reversal in Dick's fortunes.

Unfortunately, for Dick, the rumours of "gold-paved streets" proved to be without foundation and the poor country-boy became penniless. He fell victim to all sorts of charlatans and con-men that populated the streets of fourteenth century London, but he always made sure that his faithful cat was fed, often with scraps from his own plate that he could ill-afford to give away. In turn, Puss stood guard over his master as he slept and his purring kept up Dick's spirits.

Eventually, after a miserable time in the City, the two friends, one flesh, one fur, headed for home. However, when they reached Highgate Hill in north London, Dick sat down, despondently thinking about his venture. The cat tried to comfort his master, rubbing against his legs and purring loudly as though telling him not to despair and to give it one more try. It was then that Dick heard the bells of St Mary-le-Bow in the city which seemed to say to him, "Turn again, Whittington, thrice Mayor of London". And return he did, along with Puss who had given him moral support.

In the following years not only did he find his fortune but Dick Whittington became Master of the Mercers' Company, the first of the Great Twelve liveried companies in the City, and one of the wealthiest men in London. But the bells

On Highgate Hill, North London, is the Whittington Stone where young Jack is said to have heard the bells of St. Mary-le-Bow calling him back to the city. His faithful cat sits on top of the stone (left). This statue of Whittington and his cat can be seen at The Guildhall Gallery in the city (right).

The plaque on the City Church of St. Michael – Patenoster Royal. Note that he was Mayor of London not Lord Mayor.

were wrong on one point, for Dick became Mayor not three but four times. So rich and powerful did he become that he loaned money to King Henry IV and helped Henry V to finance his wars against France. It is nice to think that among all the pomp and panoply of his great office, Dick was accompanied by Puss who was now living off the fat of the land. It is claimed that this is the origin of the superstition that all black cats are lucky, especially if they cross your path.

Whittington married but had no children so he used his great wealth philanthropically, founding schools, hospitals and alms houses. When he died, his will established a trust which still administers the benefice he left to the City.

Historians, however, tells us that in the fifteenth century, tolls had to be paid for all merchandise coming into London and goods coming by water had to be trans-shipped onto smaller craft to be brought ashore. The charges for this were costly, so history has it. Whittington made his fortune by cutting out the middle-man and using his own small boats to bring cargoes to the riverside jetties. These small boats were called 'cats' and this is claimed to be the origin of Dick's feline friend. Most people would prefer Puss to be a cat rather than a boat.

So too would the Corporation of the City of London for, whatever he may be, in the Guildhall Gallery and Museum, amid statues of Cromwell, Chaucer, Shakespeare and others, is a statue of Dick Whittington and, curling round his legs, is a cat, not a small boat. And at the foot of Highgate Hill is the Whittington Stone, erected where Dick sat down with Puss and heard the bells. In 1964 a cat was added to the stone by people who believed in him. As do I, along with the many children of all ages who have enjoyed the pantomime.

A LONDON SPECIALITY

In Scotland they have haggis, a sheep's stomach bag stuffed with the heart, lungs and liver of a calf or sheep chopped with suet and onions and boiled. In Wales they have laver bread made from very fine seaweed, also known as sea-spinach which is fried in bacon fat and served, usually for breakfast, with ham or bacon and sprinkled with lemon juice. In London we have jellied eels.

At one time eels were a favourite dish of the English. In the Middle Ages, Ely, in the Fens of East Anglia, had a flourishing trade in eels which were sent to London, live, in barrels. Sometimes, rent would be paid in eel pies. The River Severn in Gloucestershire was famous for its elvers and on Easter Sunday there would be contests to see who could eat the most. Nearly all that is gone now and, in East Anglia, there is only one eel catcher left.

In London, too, there were places noted for eel pies. In Islington *The Eel Pie House* and, nearby, *Highbury Sluice*, would welcome holidaymakers who would go there especially for the dish. Eel Pie Island in the Thames near Richmond saw a flourishing trade in eel pie picnics from the seventeeth to the mid-twentieth centuries. And eel barges from Holland had been bringing their live catches up the Thames to land them at Billingsgate fish market since King Edward had granted them the right to trade in 1472.

However, the situation is different today. The trade in eels and pies has reduced to such an extent that they have become a London speciality. People think that jellied eels and eel pie, mash and liquor are only found in the East End, but at one time there were over one hundred shops in the capital. Most people know the children's nursery rhyme:

"Simple Simon met a pie man
Going to the fair."

This has its origins in Victorian London (some say earlier) when pie men with trays of pies balanced on their heads would walk the streets crying out their wares. They sold mutton or beef pies, fruit pies made with apples or cherries and, a popular favourite, eel pies which were sold with pea-soup or parsley sauce. They were not only popular because they were tasty but also because they were cheap. For London's poor, they were a rare nutritious affordable meal.

At one time there were more than 500 pie men in London but their days were numbered when the first pie shop opened in Southwark which sold pies for a penny. Shops multiplied and, eventually, the street vendors disappeared and the trade became dominated by a few families.

Pie shops used to have a standardised frontage. On either side of the door would be two large windows which used to open wide for the take-away trade. Inside, the staff would wear white aprons and hats and would serve customers who sat on wooden benches at marble-topped tables surrounded by tiled and mirrored walls. The floors the covered in saw-dust so the diners could spit out the eel bones. Everything

Manze's Eel and Pie House in Peckham.

Goddard's shop in Rotherhithe is over one hundred years old.

was spotlessly clean. In the kitchen the pies were cooked in large ovens and because they have to be cooked very soon after killing, there were tanks full of swimming eels.

There would be a limited menu: eel pie, mash and liquor; hot eels served with meat pie, mash and parsley sauce; or cold jellied eels. The gelatinous property of the bones and skins means that the dish sets well in its own jelly. Live or freshly-prepared eels were also sold to take home.

It was essentially a working-class food for artisans. Closure of the docks, rehousing of people after the Second World War and the influx and growing popularity of more exotic cuisines such as Indian and Chinese have caused the number of pie shops to fall drastically. Who knows whether this tasty, cheap and wholesome dish may become a widespread London favourite again?

PINEAPPLES, BREADFRUIT & MUTINY

Caught in the London traffic on the south end of Lambeth Bridge at the junction with the Albert Embankment, the last thing commuters think about is tropical fruit. Yet, if they were to look up at the obelisks at the end of the bridge, they would see pineapples and, perhaps, amid the idling engines, they would wonder why they were there.

The reason for these architectural decorations lies near at hand, for next to the splendid red Tudor brickwork of Lambeth Palace (London home of the Archbishops of Canterbury which, after Buckingham Palace, has the largest private garden in the capital), is the old parish church of St Mary-at-Lambeth which is now *The Garden Museum* established by the Tradescant Trust formed by two local gardeners, the Nicolsons.

The church has a long history, at one time being owned by Goda, sister of King Edward the Confessor. In the late twelfth century the living passed to Primates of All England since when it has had a varied history, being rebuilt a number of times. Finally, after severe bombing in the Second World War, it was restored in Gothic style to match the fourteenth century tower which had remained standing despite the German onslaught.

But by 1977 it had become derelict and two local gardeners, the Nicolsons, learned that it was to be

The Garden Museum at the old St Mary-at-Lambeth parish church

One of the pineapples on Lambeth Bridge (left) and Captain Bligh's tomb in the garden of St. Mary at Lambeth, see Garden Museum (right).

demolished. Knowing of its importance to horticultural history, they rallied others to form the Tradescant Trust to save it.

Like the Nicolsons, the Tradescants, father and son (both called John), were Lambeth residents and are both buried in the churchyard that now forms part of the museum. Both famous gardeners, the Tradescants were employed by the first Lord Salisbury and by King Charles I (and his Queen Henrietta Maria). Travelling far and wide in the then known world, to North Africa, North America, Russia and Europe, they brought back many new plants to England, such as the evening primrose, lilac, acacia, Virginia creeper, the cos lettuce, the plane tree that now lines London's streets and the pineapple – hence the examples on nearby Lambeth Bridge (the first was also a symbol of hospitality to the Carib Indians who placed them outside their huts as a sign of welcome).

The Tradescants were collectors of strange and wonderful things, such as a "dragon", blood that fell as rain, and a stuffed dodo – the flightless bird from the Antipodes which was so trustful of mankind that it became extinct in the seventeenth century. They kept all these oddities in a cabinet of curiosities called The Ark, which was also the name of their home which, for a small charge, was open to the public who flocked to see the bizarre things brought back from their voyages. In effect, the Ark was the first public museum and, eventually, the collection was left to the antiquary, Elias Ashmole (who died in Lambeth in 1692), and became the basis of Oxford's famous Ashmolean Museum. The Tradescants are also buried at St Mary's and

The Tradescant tomb in the Garden/Churchyard at St. Mary at Lambeth, the Garden Museum.

The commemorative plaque to John and Rosemary Nicholas, who founded the Garden Museum in 1977.

their tomb is decorated with some of the wonders seen on their travels.

Another famous Lambeth resident lies at rest there, Captain William Bligh (1754-1817), who lived at 100 Lambeth Road. In 1787 he was given command of *HMS Bounty* in order to transplant breadfruit trees from Tahiti to the West Indies. It is claimed that his harsh discipline caused mutiny when Fletcher Christian and other crew seized the ship. The Captain and 18 others were set adrift in the Pacific Ocean in a longboat. Bligh showed great navigational skill by getting the men safely to Timor, 4,000 miles away. Breadfruits were successfully transplanted when Bligh repeated the journey some years later.

The museum has displays, some permanent, others temporary, about the Tradescants, Bligh and others who brought back many of the plants we have in our gardens today. Famous gardeners, such as "Chinese" Wilson and David Douglas are remembered and there is a special display devoted to Gertrude Jekyll (1843–1932) where, besides plans and photographs, we can also see a model of her garden at Munstead Wood. There is also an extensive collection of historic garden tools, such as a seventeenth century watering pot and an eighteenth century dibber. Looking at some of these ancient artefacts, I'm glad of more recent inventions.

To the rear of the museum is a replica of a seventeenth century Knot Garden. It was designed by the Marchioness of Salisbury and is filled with plants introduced by the Tradescants, all neatly contained by attractive topiary. There are also are English cottage-garden plants and one or two exotics.

In such a place, a gardener's retreat of beauty and tranquility, the Tradescants and Captain Bligh lie serene, surrounded by Christmas Roses, Turk's Cap and Byzantine Gladiolus: not even the noise and rush of the nearby South London traffic disturbs them.

A FORTUITOUS MEETING IN DEPTFORD

When Henry VIII established the Royal Naval Dockyard in Deptford in 1513, the small Thames-side village soon became a thriving maritime town the size of Bristol, attracting all kinds of workers and craftsmen: pilots, caulkers, riggers, gunners, shipwrights and carpenters. When John Evelyn, the courtier and diarist, made his way home to Sayes Court on the evening of December 18th 1671, he saw something which amazed him. Passing a lonely, thatched cottage, he heard the sound of chisel on wood and when he looked through the window he saw, in the candlelight, a young man carving a copy of Tintoretto's painting *The Crucifixion*. Evelyn knocked and asked to see the carving and thus Grinling Gibbons was discovered.

The beauty and fine detail of the young man's work was exceptional and, eventually, Evelyn brought him to the Restoration court of King Charles II where Gibbons' reputation was established. The King was so pleased with his work that he was appointed to decorate the choir at St Paul's Cathedral and the King's dining room at Windsor where his fish, flowers, game and fruit complemented the Antonio Verrio ceiling beautifully.

Although born in Rotterdam on April 4th 1648, the son of an English draper, little is known of his early life. The exuberant and baroque nature of his work has lead people to believe that he must have studied with the Quellin family of great Flemmish carvers. Others can see his influence on work in York Minster but as he was only 22 when Evelyn discovered him, he cannot have been there long, though it may have been that he learned from the stone-masons, those skills which served him well when he made sculptures such as that of King James II in Roman garb which stands outside the National Gallery in Trafalgar Square. It may well be that working in Deptford, where he would have been surrounded by all kinds of craftsmen, including woodcarvers, influenced him. One only has to seek the magnificent door-cases of the later Georgian period in Albury Street to see what they were capable of.

Among acts of royal diplomacy is the giving of gifts, especially gifts which not only reflect the wealth and power of the giver, but also the esteem in which the recipient is held. Grinling was used by King Charles in such diplomatic exchanges. For the Grand Duke of Tuscany, Charles had him carve the magnificent Cosmino Panel, full of delicate detail, flowers, scrolls, and walnuts bursting from their shells. This limewood treasure is now in a Florentine museum.

There are certain dates in English history which everyone knows: 1066 and the Norman invasion; 1665 and the great Plague in London; and, surely one of the most memorable, 1666 and the Great Fire when much of the City of London was burned down, including 87 churches, 44 livery halls and 13,200 houses. Remarkably, less than a dozen lives were lost. London became a property

Marble font by Grinling Gibbon at St. James' Church, Piccadilly. It shows Adam and Eve and the Serpent (left) and James II – outside The National Gallery, London. Attributed to Grinling Gibbon (right)

The reredos in St. Mary's Church includes work by Grinling Gibbon. It is claimed that his 'signature' was a pea-pod, usually closed if the work had not been paid for. St. Mary's obviously paid the bill (left). Ezekiel panel, St. Nicholas Church, Deptford. The carving is of the biblical story of The Valley of Dry Bones (right).

developer's dream and, in the wake of such destruction, Sir Christopher Wren was engaged in the rebuilding of St Paul's Cathedral and other churches. He assembled craftsmen and artists such as Hawksmoor and Gibbs the architects, Thornhill the painter, Tijou the master iron-worker and Gibbons, whose task was to carve the choir-stalls and seats for the Bishop of London and the Lord Mayor. He made such a good job of it that he was appointed Master Carver to the King. With such a title and reputation, many of the nobility called upon his services and his work can be found at Chatsworth, Burghley, Petworth and Blenheim, amongst others.

It was not only the Great and the Good who used his talents for many of the Wren churches in the City got in on the act. Gibbons' work can be seen in the reredos of St Mary Abchurch, the pulpit of St Olave's, Hart Lane, the organ case at St James, Piccadilly, the altar rails at St Margaret, Lothbury and, my favourite, the exquisite font cover at All Hallows by the Tower. Of course, it does no church any harm to claim it has work by Gibbons, but because of scant evidence, lack of accounts and work done by apprentices, his work is almost as ubiquitous as the beds Good Queen Bess slept in.

Surprisingly, little of his work survives in Deptford where Evelyn discovered him. The ancient parish church of St Nicholas has a very detailed panel of the Bible story of Ezekiel and the valley of dry bones and the magnificent reredos shows many of his signature symbols, swags, festoons, doves, putti and unusually, recumbent evangelists. It is all very impressive.

A popular myth has been attached to Gibbons' work. It claims that he used the carving of a pea-pod as a signature. If the pod is open, payment has still to be made, but if it is closed, the account has been settled. A colourful example of "gilding the lily" perhaps but a good tale is all it is. Although Gibbons is known mainly for his wood carving, he was also a sculptor and examples of this type of work can be seen in St James' Church, Piccadilly, where his font shows Adam and Eve with the serpent coiled round the Tree of Life. There is also a statue of King Charles II in the Royal Hospital, Chelsea, a companion piece to the one of James II already mentioned. Critics claim that they lack the vitality of his wood carving but, as they are both "from the studio" of Grinling Gibbons, it may be that they were by apprentices. No matter, for by the time he died, aged 73 on August 3rd 1721, Grinling Gibbons had bequeathed to us enough of his splendid wood carving. Let us give thanks for Evelyn's fortuitous meeting with him one murky, damp evening in 1671.

CROYDON AIRPORT

People will find it hard today, when travelling through the urban and industrial sprawl that is Purley Way and Plough Lane in South Croydon and Wallington, to imagine that this area was the birthplace of the air transport industry. Where there are now factories, warehouses and shopping centres, there was once the official Air Terminus for London after the original civil aerodrome, Hounslow, closed.

Croydon Airport was originally two airfields. The Royal Flying Corps used Beddington Aerodrome and the National Airport Factory used Waddon Aerodrome to test aircraft. They were opened to defend London from aerial attack during the First World War.

In 1920 the two were amalgamated to make Croydon Aerodrome, London's first official customs airport. There was a drawback, however, for when aircraft had to taxi from the landing field to the hangars, the traffic in Plough Lane had to be stopped by a man with a red flag. Eventually this small drawback was remedied when the road was levelled and incorporated into the airfield.

As aviation became more important, in 1925 the Civil Aviation Board suggested enlarging Croydon airport. By 1928 it had been extended to become the new London Airport. For the first time many features now taken for

This plaque commemorates Croydon Airport Terminal.

The old Croydon Airport building which today houses the airport museum and business offices. Outside is a Morton Air Service Heron – the last flight from the airport was on September 30th 1959.

granted were provided under one roof. It had the first purpose-built terminal in the world and there were check-in desks, walk-through immigration and customs benches. No one had to be bussed to their plane for the walk to the aircraft on the apron was short – oh for those days again.

The control tower had many innovations. There were clear, extensive views; a map room; weather forecast services; and radio communications where many air traffic control procedures were first tried out and later copied by other airports as aviation developed. It is claimed that Moscow Airport terminus, which was regarded as one of the very safest, was modelled on Croydon. However, whenever there was fog, a white line was chalked across the runway to help pilots orientate themselves – an "innovation" we may smile at today.

There were some novel procedures for the passengers also. To ensure stability, they were weighed on check-in and seats were allocated accordingly. En route, five-course meals would be served on fine bone china. None of this today on budget airlines where low cost is more important than comfort and genteel travel.

While Imperial Airways dominated air traffic at Croydon, the concrete apron was extended each year to accommodate the increase in use by more and larger planes. There were small 10 passenger Handley Page W8's, 18 passenger Imperial Whitworth Argosies of 1928 and the 4-engine HP42 biplanes, all with names beginning with "H" – Hengist, Hannibal, Horatius etc. – many of which did not survive the Second World War. At first, these carried passengers to Paris, Amsterdam and other European capitals. Later they flew to further outposts of empire in Africa and India. There were Junkers-JU52's DC2's and DC3's. Air France, KLM and DLH of Germany used Croydon.

People would gather on the roof of the terminal building to see the comings and goings of film stars such as Ginger Rogers and Bob Hope and politicians such as Winston Churchill. Many spent an afternoon out having tea at the aerodrome and celebrity spotting. Such was the romance and attraction of flight that it spawned its own stars. One of the first was Bert Hinkler, the Australian pioneer aviator who, though born in Queensland, came to England in 1913 and enlisted in the Royal Naval Air Service in World War I. In 1928 he flew from England to Australia in 16 days, a new record. In his De Havilland Puss Moth he flew from the U.S.A. to the U.K. via Jamaica, Brazil and West Africa, creating more aviation records. Unfortunately, in 1933 he was killed in a solo flight to Australia when his Puss Moth crashed in the Alps.

The two biggest stars who attracted the largest crowds were Amy Johnson and Charles Lindbergh.

Amy, the young Yorkshire girl who had come to London to be secretary to a solicitor, had developed a passion for flying and wanted to prove herself in a male dominated field. She took flying lessons and became the only female ground engineer in the world. She wanted to fly solo to Australia but could find no backers. Eventually, her father and Lord Wakefield gave her the financial help. On May 5th 1930 her single-engine aircraft, *Jason*, set off from Croydon to arrive in Darwin(11,000 miles away),19 days later. She won £10,000 from the *Daily Mail* and became world famous.

On her return to Croydon on August 4th, huge crowds surged across the airfield and swarmed over the viewing platform of the control tower to greet "The Lone Girl Flyer" as she'd become known. A lunch was given in her honour, attended by Alfred Hitchcock and Noel Coward. She was aviation's Golden Girl and a national heroine.

In 1932 she married another famous British flyer, Jim Mollison, whose record for flying solo to Cape Town she went on to break. Eventually, she gave up long distance flying but in World War II she joined the British Air Transport Authority and in 1941 she ditched over the Thames and was drowned.

On May 19th 1924, Charles Lindbergh, the young American pilot flew across the Atlantic in 33 hours, landing his Ryan monoplane, *The Sprit of St Louis* in Paris. He became an international hero and when he flew to Croydon on May 27th 1927, a crowd of over 100,000 met him. Other planes couldn't land and one had to make an emergency landing it a South Croydon field.

In August 1939, as war approached, there was much activity in Croydon. On August 25th the R.A.F. began to arrive. Shortly afterwards a Junkers JU52 D-Axis was the last German plane to leave Croydon and by the 28th most of the Lufthansa staff had gone. On August 30th R.A.F. Croydon was established and on September 1st all civil functions stopped.

In 1940 during the Battle of Britain, Croydon became the target of the first major bombing raid on London. It remained an RAF airfield for the remainder of the war. It has the distinction of being the only frontline defensive British airfield in both World Wars.

After the War, the Government decided that, along with Northolt, Croydon would be used as one of the two London airports. However, in 1944 the Ministry of Civil Aviation acquired Heathrow as a site for a new London airport and this, together with the development of Gatwick, meant that Croydon's days were numbered. The two new airfields could take the new, larger aircraft which Croydon could not. On September 30th 1959 a Morton Air Service Heron to Rotterdam was the last flight from Croydon Airport, the first international air terminal.

MID-WINTER CELEBRATIONS
IN THE BOROUGH

January 6th, usually associated by many with "twelve lords a-leaping", is the Feast of the Epiphany when the Magi, the three Wise Men, arrived at Bethlehem with their gifts, gold, frankincense and myrrh for the Christ child. It is also the day which celebrates the baptism of Jesus. Many countries make this day their chief celebration, rather than Christmas Day. In the Orthodox Church it is the Feast of the Incarnation when Christ was made known to the world. In Spain the 6th is known as *"Los Tres Reyes" (The Three Kings).*

How many realise that Twelfth Night replaced a more ancient traditional midwinter festival, such as the Roman Saturnalia? While Prince Albert introduced us to fir trees and the sending of cards, his wife, Queen Victoria, thought Twelfth Night too pagan and had it removed from the calendar of holidays. It may have been the topsy-turvy nature of this Feast of Fools that upset Her Majesty. Perhaps she was not amused when the usual order of things was changed and accepted norms were upset. During this Feast, a Lord of Misrule was appointed, for example a choirboy could be made a bishop and a bishop would become a chorister. Servants could play tricks on their lords and ladies who would serve them at table rather than the other way round. In the Armed

Forces such role reversal can still be seen when the officers wait on the other ranks at Christmas Dinner.

Watered-down remnants of such pagan rituals remain with us. Often the Lord of Misrule would be chosen if he found a pea or a bean in his slice of special "Bean Cake" and then he would be crowned with a paper crown. Today we hide tokens in our Christmas puddings and we wear silly paper hats, often crowns.

Before Prince Albert introduced pine trees into our homes in 1840, very often an evergreen branch was decorated with candles, sweetmeats and ribbons. Revellers would kiss and make wishes under "the Kissing Tree". This could be the origin of kissing under the mistletoe.

Plants associated with this winter feast, holly and ivy, also have pre-Christmas connections. The Romans used holly in their Saturnalia celebrations, making fire with it which would burn brightly even when wet. The black berries of ivy were thought to keep away demons.

"Wassailing" (from the Anglo-Saxon "*was hael*", meaning "be healthy") was also an important tradition. A bowl of hot ale and spices would be passed around and carried into neighbours' homes, accompanied by men waving green branches – "wassailing among the leaves so green". Now we serve mulled wine or bowls of punch and play charades, echoes of the Feast of Fools.

This, the darkest time of year, is when folk plays were performed, usually called "mummings", they would have traditional characters such as Father Christmas, St George, a doctor and others. Common to both Christian and pagan mummers' plays is the theme of death and resurrection.

Father Christmas in front of Shakespeare's Globe Theatre on Bankside as part of the Twelfth Night Celebration (left). The Green Man leads the revellers to story-telling and mulled wine in Borough Market (right).

On January 6th, or the Sunday or Bank Holiday nearest to it, near the Globe Theatre on London's Bankside, "the Lion's Part", a group of actors specialising in verse drama, celebrate Twelfth Night with a play full of fun and games, colour and music. St George wins his sword-fight; the

Green Man, a fertility figure common to many cultures and known to many from pub signs, appears from the Thames, usually accompanied by flaming torches; Father Christmas, glorious in scarlet robes, tinsel and holly crown and with a magnificent white beard also arrives, much to the joy of children in the watching crowd. There are tabors, a fiddle, an accordion, a cock-horse and a sword fight: all good clean fun, much appreciated by the onlookers who are encouraged to learn the farandole as they progress first to Borough Market for more fun and games and then on to The George in Borough High Street, the last remaining galleried inn, for more celebrations.

Queen Victoria was not the only one to find such jollification out of order for during the Interregnum, the Puritan parliament cancelled Christmas and it was not until the restoration of King Charles II that it was legally revived. Shakespeare's *Twelfth Night* was first performed on January 6th 1602 at Middle Temple Hall. Let's not forget the Feast of Fools again.

GRAVE PLEASURES

Early nineteenth century inner London burial grounds were in a parlous state: they were so full that bodies were buried in graves so shallow that any scavenging animal could uncover them. They were a ready source of income for grave robbers and body snatchers. Such was the outcry that Parliament was petitioned and between 1837 and 1841, six cemeteries were established on greenfield sites outside the city boundaries in Kensal Green, Highgate, Brompton, Abbey Park, Nunhead and the hamlet of Norwood.

The West Norwood Cemetery was formed when the South Metropolitan Cemetery Company bought 40 acres of land in the fields and wooded hills around the small village that has since become a London suburb. Apart from paths and the local unsurfaced track through the village, there was no major transport route nearby and all the funerals were by horse-drawn hearse followed by the carriages of the mourners and those on foot. When the Baptist Minister, the Rev, Charles Haddon Spurgeon died in 1892, his funeral was attended by more mourners than any other in the history of the cemetery, most of them on foot and, presumably, many of them had attended his services at the Metropolitan Tablernacle where his "magnificent voice and command of pure idiomatic Saxon English" attracted huge congregations.

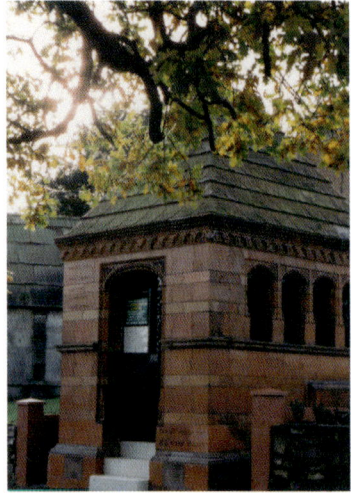

*The grave of Mrs Beeton (left) and the tomb of Sir Henry Tate
and his family (right)*

The cemetery became, for South London, North Surrey and Kent, the fashionable place to be buried.

In 1842 the Brotherhood of the Greek Community in London (wealthy merchants, many of whom had fled persecution in the Ottoman Empire), bought five acres of the cemetery. In 1872 they enlarged it, making a most remarkable cemetery within a cemetery. Grand tombs and mausolea were built, perhaps the most impressive of which is the mortuary chapel, a handsome Greek Doric style building, built in memory of Augustus Ralli who died at Eton in 1872. This chapel has a beautiful ceiling which is richly coffered in blue and gold.

Over the next century or so, and before it followed the fate of its inner London predecessors, West Norwood Cemetery became the resting ground for many famous people. Perhaps the most famous grave is that of Isabella Beeton (1836-1865), whose book *Mrs Beeton's Book of Household Management*, with its 3,000 recipes and countless hints for running a Victorian household, was a huge success selling more than 60,000 copies in its first year. She died young, being only 29, of puerperal fever.

The tomb of Sir Henry Doulton (1820-1897) is a handsome mausoleum in redbrick and terracotta tiles, presumably from his riverside factory in nearby Lambeth. There used to be Doulton vases inside but these have sadly been stolen.

Close by is another terracotta mausoleum, that of art collector, philanthropist and Unitarian, Sir Henry Tate (1819-1899) whose invention of the sugar cube made him a huge fortune and lead to the formation of the Tate Gallery and a number of libraries in south London.

Nearby is the grave of Sir Henry Bessemer (1813-1898) whose process of converting cast iron in to steel revolutionised steel manufacture by not only reducing production costs, but making it possible to use steel where previously only cast iron had been strong enough.

Baron Julius de Reuter (1816-1899) first realised the importance of collecting and transmitting telegraphic news and established his news agency in London, at the Royal Exchange, in 1851. His grave is marked by a pink granite monument.

Many wealthy and influential Victorians whose names are still remembered today are in West Norwood, but also lying there are those who were famous in their time for things more ephemeral than steel, cubed sugar or pottery.

The prize-fighter, Tom Spring (1795-1851), the Champion of England, lies beneath a monument showing a lion lying down with a lamb, now, alas, somewhat worn away and covered in ivy. His bare-fist fights attracted thousands and he was so famous in his day that a weekly newspaper was named after him, *Tom Spring's Sporting Chronicle.*

William Dufton (1830-1877) was a famous billiard-player who won £1,000 in one match – a huge amount then. His other claim to fame was that he taught the Prince of Wales to play billiards. Was Queen Victoria amused by that? Dufton commited suicide and is buried in a common grave.

That great institution of Victorian life, the Music Hall, is also represented. Fred Kitchen (1872-1951) was a famous comedian on the halls. He was part of Fred Karno's troupe and, at one time, he worked with Charlie Chaplin. Much of Kitchen's humour was visual; with his large feet and bandy legs, his walk always raised a laugh and, some said, was the origin of Chaplin's Little Tramp's walk.

James Bassett (1854-1907) whose stage name was Charles Bertram, was a leading conjuror on the Victorian stage. Not only was he popular with audiences but also with His Royal Highness the Prince of Wales, to whom he bore a marked resemblance. He appeared before the Royal Household many times and earned the title "the King's Conjurer".

Beneath the Dissenters' chapel, now demolished, are the catacombs. Although almost abandoned, they are dry, well-ventilated and there are some lights. The central aisle contains an ingenious piece of machinery, a hydraulic catafalque which silently brought the coffins down from the chapel above. The machine now is rusty and covered with spider-webs and droppings. From this aisle, others run off, stacked with coffins. If a body was to be deposited in the catacombs, it had to be encased in lead, then placed in a coffin which was covered in either satin or leather (on which many fine patterns were made with nails). Some coffins still have leather tatters hanging from them. The catacombs were intended to contain 2,000 coffins.

In the early 80's criminals found it attractive for storing their drug hauls, for what better place was there for their nefarious activities than large, secure, rent free underground premises where no-one wants to go? Stories of ghosts and spectres have always been associated with graveyards and it was someone talking of "eerie" noises and "spooky" lights coming from the cemetery that alerted the police and eventually bought the drug runners to their end.

Since taking over in 1966, Lambeth Council have done much not only to restore the cemetery to a semblance of its previous grandeur, but also to bring the ecological value of such places in built-up areas to the public's attention. There is also a wide variety of shrubs and trees and in Spring daffodils and primroses flourish. There is wildlife also, the cemetery being home to foxes, squirrels and owls. Kestrels nest on the pediment of the Greek mortuary chapel. In Egyptian mythology, a hawk is one of the forms a disembodied person might adopt when visiting his body after mummification. What an appropriate visitor.

ROTHERHITHE: MORE THAN JUST A TUNNEL

Go east from Tower Bridge, along the south bank of the Thames, past Butler's Wharf, Tea Trade Wharf, Amber Wharf and all those other reminders of our rich mercantile past, now converted to smart and expensive dwellings, and you will come to that part of Southwark which is London postal district SE16, once called Redriff but now known as Rotherhithe.

The name is ancient, from two Saxon words, *"retha"* meaning "a mariner" and *"hythe"* "a landing place", though there are some who say it means "a landing place from where cattle are shipped". Whatever the origin, Rotherhithe has a long and rich history: Roman bricks were found in the church; King Canute is thought to have begun his trench to bypass London here; King Edward III had a moated manor house next to the river; John of Gaunt, his son, had a fleet fitted out here and Henry IV got over a bout of leprosy here.

The River Thames is liquid history and where its banks are now lined with apartment blocks, there would once have been traders and many kinds of ships, even warships. Their masts would have soared above the dwellings of caulkers, carvers, carpenters, captains and other associated crafts. The river was the life-blood of the community.

Johnathan Swift's Lemuel Gulliver hailed from Rotherhithe; Samuel Pepys records in his diary, going down river to the Cherry Gardens to taste the fruit and to promenade there; and J.M.W. Turner, from the same garden, painted *The Fighting Téméraire*, a Trafalgar battleship, being towed up-river to be broken. Many ships of the Georgian navy and the East India Company were built at this riverside village.

Such a full and colourful past needed hostelries to *vittel* it and perhaps the two most famous in Rotherhithe are *The Angel* and *The Mayflower*. The monks of Bermondsey Priory founded the former in the fifteenth century, offering hospitality to travellers, many of whom were on their way to the shrine of St Thomas á Becket at Canterbury, and others came for health reasons – to drink at the nearby chalybeate springs. Captain Cook spent time there preparing for his epic voyage to Australia. Hanging Judge Jeffreys (1648-1689) would watch from *The Angel* those he had condemned to be hung at Execution Dock across the river in Poplar; some claim his ghost haunts the balcony which overhangs the Thames and the trapdoors through which smugglers and river pirates would hoist their stolen goods.

The Mayflower, dating from the 1500's was originally called *The Spread Eagle*, but was renamed after the ship which took the Pilgrim Fathers to America in 1520. Captain Christopher Jones, master of the ship and a local man, favoured the inn. Like *The Angel*, it too has splendid river views and is the only pub licensed to sell American postal stamps.

The area had its share of n'er-do-wells and rogues. Perhaps one of the most famous was Moll Cutpurse, born

Mary Firth in 1589. She dressed as a man, smoked a pipe and was a successful pickpocket, hence her nickname. She graduated to highway robbery on Blackheath and was even in the Parliamentary Army in the English Civil War.

Though she was eventually captured and spent some time in Newgate Gaol, she bribed her way out and died, in 1662, safely in her own home at the good age, for those days, of 75.

The centre of the village, both actually and metaphorically, is the parish church of Rotherhithe, St Mary's. Although the present building is Georgian, being built in 1715 (with the tower added in 1747), there was a church here in Saxon times and below those remains are, it has been said, Roman bricks. There has been Christian worship on this site for over a thousand years.

It's a handsome, spacious building, the barrel of the roof being supported by four massive wooden beams enclosed in plaster to make them look like pillars. The delicately covered reredos are claimed to have been the work of Grinling Gibbons (1648-1721) who, before he was discovered by John Evelyn, lived and worked at nearby Deptford.

Other woodwork of note includes the Communion Table and the two Bishop's Chairs, made from wood of *The Téméraire*, a 104 gun battleship which took part in the Battle of Trafalgar and ended her days in a Rotherhithe breaker's yard.

In the churchyard there is a grave of Prince Lee Boo, son of the Rupack or King of the Palau islands in the Pacific Ocean, south east of the Phillipines. In 1783,

In St. Mary's Church, Rotherhithe, is the statue of one of the Indians who helped the first colonist through their first winter in the New World (left). The Mayflower Inn, Rotherhithe (right)

Captain Wilson and the crew of *The Antelope*, an East India Company packet, were wrecked on those islands. Not only were the inhabitants friendly but they helped Captain Wilson to repair his ship. In return, the Englishman aided the King against his enemies and Wilson bought the prince back to England and Rotherhithe to be educated, as his father requested.

Not only was Loe Boo impressed by nearly all he saw, but those he came into contact with were impressed by him, his friendliness and ability. He became a great favourite in the Wilson household where he lived. Unfortunately, in 1784 he died in one of the outbreaks of smallpox that London was susceptible to. He was given a grand funeral and buried in St Mary's churchyard. A nice touch was that in

1912, the then London County Council renamed a nearby street "Rupack Street" in memory not only of Lee Boo, but also of his father and the people of the Palau islands, now the Republic of Palau, who had aided the sailors of *The Antelope* all those years before.

When thinking of the area, most people think of the tunnel carrying road traffic north and south of the river between Rotherhithe and Shadwell, built in 1904-8 and opened by the Duke and Duchess of York, the future King George V and Queen Mary. However, next to St Mary's Church is an older, and at one time more famous tunnel. Between 1825-1842 Sir Marc Brunel and his son, Isambard Kingdom Brunel, built what was one of the world's great engineering feats, the first underwater tunnel. Although this was intended as a road tunnel, it became a pedestrian thoroughfare instead. It was not the hoped for success and, in 1869, it was converted to a tunnel for the East London line of the London Underground system. The oldest section of the oldest underground in the world and Brunel's Engine House, built to pump out water, still stands and is open to visitors on weekend afternoons.

The docks were the working part of Rotherhithe for hundreds of years. Howland Great Docks, one of the largest on the river was built in about 1700 but its name was changed to Greenland Dock when the whaling industry became important. The timber trade also became established as is shown in the names of other docks – Canada, Russia and Norway – where the timber originated. This also accounts for Swedish and Finnish churches in

Rotherhithe; right beside the road, is the Norwegian church with its Viking longboat weather-vane. These churches act as community centres for their nationals who live in London.

The docks took a battering in the Second World War and while many were rebuilt afterwards, by 1970 the development of container trade meant that industry moved down-river where there was more room and the last of Rotherhithe's docks closed. While the former dock areas have been regenerated, the rich historical roots of the area are worth investigating: go explore, Rotherhithe is more than just a tunnel.

TURNER, BLAKE & BENEDICT
ARNOLD IN BATTERSEA

Say "Battersea" and most people will think of two things: the "Temporary Home for Lost and Starving Dogs" founded in 1860 my Mrs Mary Tealby or Sir Giles Gilbert Scott's 1937 Power Station, of which all that remains today are the four fluted chimneys and retaining walls. There is much more to the transpontine postal districts of SW8 and SW11.

Battersea had its origins in the low-lying marshy areas surrounding "Beatrice's Edge" or "Patrick's island", first mentioned in A.D.63 as belonging to the Abbess of Barking. While there may have been some Saxon settlement, objects such as the magnificent Battersea Shield, now in the British Museum, show that there was earlier occupation.

For centuries it remained a riverside village, upstream from the capital and was centred on Battersea Square, today a trendy spot with wine bars and restaurants where, weather permitting, you can dine *alfresco* beneath a canopy of trees.

To the north of the square on a promontory overlooking the Thames is St Mary's Church, surely one of the most charming and most attractively placed riverside churches. There has been a church here since Norman times and St Mary's is mentioned in The Doomsday Book. The present church dates from 1777 and has recently, and most satisfyingly, been refurbished and redecorated in Georgian colours.

The stained glass indicates a wealth of famous associations. The east window depicts Margaret Beaufort (mother of Henry VII), Henry VIII and Elizabeth I, all royal connections of the most important local family, the St Johns. A window celebrates the marriage here of William Blake (1757-1827), poet and painter, to a local girl, Catherine Boucher, who signed the register with an "X".

Another window shows the artist J.M.W. Turner (1775-1851). It is claimed that it was from here that he painted some of those pictures showing the interaction of light on water, such as sunsets on the Thames. The eighteenth century botanist William Curtis (1749-1799) has a window dedicated to him. He had gardens along the river at Bermondsey and Lambeth, became director of the Chelsea Physic Garden and published the *Botanical Magazine* which continues today as the *Kew Magazine*. The area had become a centre of market gardening and was famous for such things as asparagus and lavender (Lavender Hill is a well-known thoroughfare) and Curtis may have found this useful for his studies).

Perhaps the most unexpected stained glass window is that dedicated to Benedict Arnold (1741-1801) the American general and turncoat who defected to the British in the American Revolution. He fled to England after the war, lived nearby and died in obscurity. The window was installed by Americans, to promote peaceful understanding between nations and in the spirit of letting bygones be bygones.

St. Mary's church, Battersea.

Nearby, in Vicarage Crescent, is another architectural and historical gem – one of the few remaining grand houses in the village, Old Battersea House, dating from

1699. Built on Tudor foundations, some claim it is by Sir Christopher Wren. This handsome house stands in what little remains of the extensive grounds (once surrounded by lavender fields, but today surrounded by blocks of flats). It has had many uses since its last private occupation in the early nineteenth century by Sir John Shaw Lefevre, a barrister who established the Colony of Australia. In 1930 it ended up as a school before Battersea Council bought it and were going to demolish it. Such was the outcry, that it was saved by an Act of Parliament. Colonel Charles Stirling and his wife, sister of the painter Evelyn de Morgan, became tenants, bringing with them the De Morgan collection of pre-Raphaelite paintings and pottery. Mrs Stirling, who died at almost 100 years of age, bequeathed the collection to the De Morgan Foundation. In 1971 the house, which was somewhat dilapidated, was shown to the American millionaire publisher Malcom Forbes who negotiated a 99 year lease with the Borough of Wandsworth. The house was restored and is now home to the Forbes Magazine Collection of Victorian Paintings. Few who rush by on the road outside realise what a treasure house lies behind the high wall. The De Morgan Collection of Pottery was moved to the West Hill Library in Wandsworth on his death in 1990.

Almost next door are the two remaining eighteenth century houses Devonshire House and, at No.42, the Vicarage. In the latter, lived Edward Wilson (1872-1912) the naturalist and explorer. He first went with Robert Falcon Scott on *The Discovery* to the Antarctic in 1900-1904, returning on the *Terra Nova* on its fateful voyage in 1910. Wilson was one of the five men who reached the South Pole only to find that the Norwegian explorer Roald Amundsen had beaten them to it. All five died on the journey back to base.

*The memorial windows to the painter J.M.W. Turner (left)
and the poet William Blake (right)*

If you walk eastwards along the Thameside Path past the church, you will come to the Albert Bridge which is the prettiest bridge on the river, with its pastel hues, lit up at night by hundreds of bulbs. Built in 1871-1873 by R.M. Ordish, notices at both ends tell soldiers to break step when crossing the bridge in case rhythmic vibrations have an untoward effect. The Millennium Bridge had a similar problem!

Continuing across Albert Bridge Road is Battersea Park, remembered by many as one of the sites of the Festival of Britain in 1951. However, the area has a long and, at times, less salubrious reputation. Some claim that it was here that Julius Caesar crossed the Thames to conquer the Catevellauni. In 1671, Thomas Blood the Irish adventurer and Parliamentarian, hid in the bulrushes to assassinate

King Charles II as he bathed. He later claimed that it was "awe of majesty" that prevented him. The King must have admired the man's audacity for not only did he pardon him for that and his later theft of the Crown Jewels from the Tower, but he also restored his lands!

In 1829, Battersea Fields was the scene of a duel between the Duke of Wellington and the Earl of Winchilsea who had slighted the Duke's honour. When the second gave the order to fire, Winchilsea never raised his arm and the Duke, seeing this, fired into the air. Winchilsea then fired wide and apologised. Honour was satisfied.

Over the years fairs were held on the fields attracting huge crowds and all sorts of riff-raff. Cut-purses and footpads frequented the area and the place became so notorious for lawlessness and raucous behaviour that the Government was forced to act. In 1846 an Act was passed enabling the creation of a public park in Battersea which, after much work and many improvements, was opened in 1853. It followed a long tradition of riverside pleasure gardens such as Ranelagh, Cremorne and Vauxhall and remains a popular "green lung" with many visitors, more so now that Battersea has become fashionable.

There's more to Battersea than people realise and it's well worth a visit. Do go!

SANCTUARY

"The Lundenwic and Thorney Island Area of Special Archaeological Priority". What a mouthful! And where is this area? It is somewhere known by millions whose feet tread its streets and enter its buildings daily; whose cameras take snaps by the thousands. It is Parliament Square and environs. Just think how much of our history is concentrated in those few acres: the Palace of Westminster (a.k.a. Houses of Parliament), Westminster Abbey, St Margaret's Church, Methodist Central Hall, the Treasury (ironically built on what was once Thieving Lane). The numerous statues there include Winston Churchill, David Lloyd George, Abraham Lincoln, Nelson Mandela to mention but a few, and the Middlesex Guildhall, now the Supreme Court.

The whole area was originally part of the grounds of the Collegiate Church of Saint Peter, built by Edward the Confessor on the marshy Thorney Island and better known as Westminster Abbey. Much of it was a place of sanctuary which was originally the consecrated area in a church, usually around the alter, where a saint's bones were often buried or some other holy relic interred. Eventually, the concept was extended to cover areas outside the church building itself and became a place where people could claim asylum and were safe from arrest. To remove someone from a place of sanctuary was tantamount to committing sacrilege and those who did so could be excommunicated. It was King Ethelbert (ruled from 561-616) who introduced the concept of sanctuary into English law in about AD600 and it lasted over a thousand years in England until King James I abolished it in 1623.

Originally, the concept of sanctuary had been designed by the Church to protect the weak and prevent government by whim, revenge or oppression. However, it was not extended to everyone. Those who were non-Christian, traitors or who had committed sacrilege were denied it.

The whole precinct of Westminster Abbey was a sanctuary at one time. However, over the centuries, especially since it was abolished by King James I, the area has shrunk to the patch of lawn to the north of the building where the Field of Poppies is laid out in November and to three street names, Little Sanctuary, Broad Sanctuary and The Sanctuary.

Not only was the open area of the precinct sanctuary but a fortified tower which was the main bastion of safety once stood on the site of the Supreme Court. This large stone keep, two stories high and with heavy oak doors, saw some interesting residents over the years.

Perhaps the most famous was Elizabeth Woodville, Queen to King Edward IV. The Wars of the Roses (1455-1485), that complex struggle between the Houses of York and Lancaster, saw power swing back and forth between the two and Elizabeth was caught up in these vacillations. Twice she had to flee to the abbey and take sanctuary. In 1740, when the Lancastrians had the upper hand, she

One of three street names which are all that remain to indicate the Sanctuary Precinct of Westminister Abbey (left) and The Supreme Court, previously the Middlesex Guildhall. On this site once stood the Scantuary Tower

went there with her family until her husband was restored to the throne. It was while there this first time that Edward, their first son, and heir to the throne, was born. When her husband, King Edward IV died in 1483, she fled there again, this time taking her increased family of five

daughters and a younger son, Richard, Duke of York. Lest it be thought that living in sanctuary was an uncomfortable existence, it is claimed that Elizabeth brought so much furniture with her that holes had to be knocked in the walls to get it in.

Her first son, who was by right, King Edward V, was not with her, having been seized by his uncle, Richard of Gloucester who claimed to be looking after his nephew's interests. The wily Duke managed to persuade both the

Queen and the Archbishop of Canterbury that it would be in the younger son's interests and safety to be a companion to his older brother and be 'protected' by his loving uncle. The two young princes were kept in the Tower of London but only briefly, for once they entered that Norman stronghold, they were never seen again. So much for sanctuary!

Another person with Royal connections who sought sanctuary at Westminster was John Skelton, the Poet Laureate, who at one time was tutor to King Henry VIII. His wit and coarse comedy made him enemies as well as friends at court and he was imprisoned a number of times before eventually falling out with the then power behind the throne, Cardinal Wolsey. He was no man to make an enemy of and Skelton fled to the Sanctuary Tower at the abbey. It is claimed that he died there. He is buried in nearby St Margaret's church.

Sanctuary for crime was abolished in 1623 but the Sanctuary Tower was not demolished until later in the seventeenth century and the Supreme Court now stands on the site . . . another type of sanctuary, perhaps.

MADNESS, WAR AND PEACE
IN SOUTHWARK

After the City of London, the Thameside Borough of Southwark is the oldest in the capital. It's a densely populated area, not just with 250,000 inhabitants, but also with those commuters who come there daily to work. Open space is a premium.

One such invaluable open space in the north-west of the borough is the 6 hectare Geraldine Mary Harmsworth Park. This area once known as St George's Fields was low-lying marsh, criss-crossed by streams. In the sixteenth century the herbalist John Gerard (1545-1611) collected water violets there.

The park was popular, especially on Sundays, with locals who took their leisure there. Troop manoeuvres were sometimes held on the Fields and it was notorious as a meeting place for disaffected assemblies which often became riots. One such was in 1780 when the anti-catholic Gordon rioters, 50,000 strong began their march on Parliament from there. What started out as a demonstration against the repeal of anti-Roman Catholic legislation degenerated into looting and pillaging in which 850 people were killed. The Bank of England was attacked and the clerks melted down their own lead ink wells when they ran out of ammunition.

The Buddhist Peace Garden: The plants are from the Himalayan region of Tibet.

At the centre of the Tibetan Peace Garden is the bronze cast of the Kalachakra Mandala; it is holy and has the power to confer its blessings on all who see it. His Holiness, the Dalai Lama, considers it to be a potent "vehicle for world peace".

By the late eighteenth century the land was drained and the area became "gentrified". Captain Bligh of *Bounty* fame lived across the road and in the early nineteenth century, Charlie Chaplin lived in the area which, by then, had gone downhill.

In 1815 the Royal Bethlehem Hospital moved to the site. "Bedlam", for most people is synonymous with "chaos and disorder". They are unaware that it is a corruption of "Bethlehem" and its origins in the Priory of St Mary of Bethlehem which was founded in London in 1247, though it wasn't until the fourteenth century that it became a hospital for "distracted" patients, as they were known at the time.

Before arriving south of the river, the hospital had other homes in the City, though the first, at Bishopsgate, was just outside the walls of the Square Mile. Intended for 20 patients, it soon became overcrowded and in 1676 moved to a splendid new building designed by Robert Hooke at Moorfields. The public attitude towards mental illness was far from sympathetic; in the eighteenth century the mad were seen as public entertainment. "Let's go see the lunatics", was a common invitation to diversion and sightseers would stroll up and down the long galleries at Moorfields, amused by the antics of the inmates. The Duke of Cumberland, "Butcher" Cumberland, so called because of the viciousness of his reprisals after the Jacobite Rebellion of 1745, ended up here and Dr Johnson records seeing him frantically rearranging the straw he slept on time and time again.

In 1815, once again, the hospital moved, this time to St George's Fields where there was much improvement: large windows let in more light, flowers and plants were placed in the wards and song-birds and animals were allowed. Richard Dadd (1817-1886) the painter was here as was Edward Oxford who tried to assassinate Queen Victoria. However, when Broadmoor, the first state Criminal Lunatic Asylum was opened in 1864, the criminally insane were transferred there.

In 1930 the hospital was moved again, this time to Monks Orchard, a country estate in Beckenham where there was more space, light and fresh air – green leafy therapy for all. There was great concern that the Southwark site might be built upon. Viscount Rothermere bought the estate and gave it to the London City Council for a public park in memory of his mother, Geraldine Mary Harmsworth, and there was great delight when it was opened to the public in 1934. The old hospital had been demolished except for the central section which became the Imperial War Museum, which tells the story of conflict during the twentieth century, in exhibitions and displays. It is a popular museum, attracting over 500,000 visitors a year.

Southwark Council and its team of Ranger Gardeners now manage the rest of the park which has more to it than just a history of madness and all things martial. In 1999 the Tibet foundation, in association with the council, created a Tibetan Peace Garden in the north-east corner which serves a number of purposes: as a constant reminder of the need for peace; to create greater awareness of Bhuddist culture; to contribute to understanding between East and West; as a testament to the courage of the Tibetan people; and as a place of peace and tranquillity where anyone can contemplate – in fact, the name *"Samten Kyil"*, which it is called, means "Garden of Contemplation".

The Imperial War Museum in Lambeth, site of the third Bethlehem Hospital, with the barrels of a World War I gun in front.

At the entrance to the garden is a language pillar which has, carved in four languages (Tibetan, English, Hindi and Chinese), the Dalai Lama's message of peace and armony. His Holiness opened the garden on May 13th 1999. At the centre of the inner circle is a bronze cast of the Kalachackra Mandala, the Wheel of Time, which has the power to confer blessings on all who see it.

East meets west on the outer perimeter of the circle for four contemporary sculptures, carved in Portland stone by Hamish Horsley, represent the elements: Air, Fire Earth and Water. Other Buddhists ideas, such as the Noble Eightfold Path, the Eight Auspicious Symbol and the Six Perfections are also represented. Around them all, and leading up the garden, are shrubs, flowers and plants associated with Tibet and the Himalayas.

In front of the Imperial War Museum are two huge 15ft guns from the First World War, from *HMS Resolution* and *HMS Ramilies*, and there, in their shadow, lies the Buddhist Peace Garden; an ironic and deliberate juxtaposition to remind us all of the need for more of one and less of the other.